Catherine Owen

Catherine Owen's New Cook Book ..

Catherine Owen

Catherine Owen's New Cook Book ..

ISBN/EAN: 9783744786232

Printed in Europe, USA, Canada, Australia, Japan

Cover: Foto ©Andreas Hilbeck / pixelio.de

More available books at **www.hansebooks.com**

CATHERINE OWEN'S

NEW COOK BOOK

Part I.
CULTURE AND COOKING
OR, ART IN THE KITCHEN

Part II.
PRACTICAL RECIPES

BY

CATHERINE OWEN
(Mrs. Nitsch)

NEW YORK
CASSELL & COMPANY, Limited
739 & 741 BROADWAY

PREFACE TO NEW EDITION.

In the first part of this book I endeavored to help inexperienced housekeepers in the difficulties they find in using even the best recipes without some knowledge of cooking. In response, however, to a general demand for more recipes in "Culture and Cooking," I have prepared a second part to be used in conjunction with it. In this addition, I have tried, not so much to give a great many recipes, as to give the best I know of each kind, all tested by myself, and to give them so minutely that they will be easily practiced. Where there are many ways of cooking one thing I have given two recipes, the finest I know, and one more simple.

I have tried to avoid repeating in this second part of the book, the information contained in the first, except in the one or two instances where I have thought repetition of a rule may have the effect of successive blows of the hammer on a nail—drive it home.

THE AUTHOR.

PREFACE.

This is not a cookery book. It makes no attempt to replace a good one; it is rather an effort to fill up the gap between you and your household oracle, whether she be one of those exasperating old friends who maddened our mother with their vagueness, or the newer and better lights of our own generation, the latest and best of all being a lady as well known for her novels as for her works on domestic economy—one more proof, if proof were needed, of the truth I endeavor to set forth —if somewhat tediously forgive me—in this little book: that cooking and cultivation are by no means antagonistic. Who does not remember with affectionate admiration Charlotte Brontë taking the eyes out of the potatoes stealthily, for fear of hurting the feelings of her purblind old servant; or Margaret Fuller shelling peas?

The chief difficulty, I fancy, with women trying recipes is, that they fail and know not why they fail, and so become discouraged, and this is where I hope to step in. But although this is not a cookery book, insomuch as it does not deal chiefly with recipes, I shall yet give a few; but only when they are, or I believe them to be, better than those in general use, or good things little known, or supposed to belong to the domain of a French *chef*, of which I have introduced a good many. Should I succeed in making things that were obscure before clear to a few women, I shall be as proud as was Mme. de Genlis when she boasts in her Memoirs that she has taught six new dishes to a German housewife. Six new dishes! When Brillat-Savarin says: "He who has invented *one* new dish has done more for the pleasure of mankind than he who has discovered a star."

CONTENTS.

PART I.

CHAPTER I.

PAGE

PRELIMINARY REMARKS.................................... 1

CHAPTER II.

ON BREAD.

Sponge for bread.—One cause of failure.—Why home-made bread often has a hard crust.—On baking.—Ovens.—More reasons why bread may fail to be good.—Light rolls.—Rusks.—Kreuznach horns.—Kringles.—Brioche (Paris Jockey Club recipe).—Soufflée bread.—A novelty........ 12

CHAPTER III.

PASTRY.

Why you fail in making good puff paste.—How to succeed.—How to handle it.—To put fruit pies together so that the syrup does not boil out.—Ornamenting fruit pies.—Rissolettes.—Pastry tablets.—Frangipane tartlets.—Rules for ascertaining the heat of your oven...................... 22

CHAPTER IV.

WHAT TO HAVE IN YOUR STORE-ROOM.

Mushroom powder (recipe).—Stock to keep, or glaze (recipe).—Uses of glaze.—Glazing meats, hams, tongues, etc.—Maître d'hôtel butter (recipe).—Uses of it.—Ravigotte or Montpellier butter (recipe).—Uses of it.—Roux.—Blanc (recipes).—Uses of both.—Brown flour, its uses.......... 28

CHAPTER V.

LUNCHEONS.

Remarks on what to have for luncheons.—English meat pies.—Windsor pie.—Veal and ham pie.—Chicken pie.—Raised pork pie.—(Recipes).—Ornamenting meat pies.—Galantine (recipe).—Fish in jelly.—Jellied oysters.—A new mayonnaise luncheon for small families.—Potted meats (recipes).—Anchovy butter.—A new omelet.—Potato snow.—Lyonnaise potatoes 35

CHAPTER VI.

A CHAPTER ON GENERAL MANAGEMENT IN VERY SMALL FAMILIES.

How to have little dinners.—Hints for bills of fare, etc.—Filet de bœuf Chateaubriand (recipe).—What to do with the odds and ends.—Various recipes.—Salads.—Recipes 47

CHAPTER VII.

FRYING.

Why you fail.—Panure or bread-crumbs, to prepare.—How to prepare flounders as filets de sole.—Fried oysters.—To clarify dripping for frying.—Remarks.—Pâte à frire à la Carême.—Same, à la Provençale.—Broiling............. 55

CHAPTER VIII.

Roasting 62

CHAPTER IX.

BOILING AND SOUPS.

Boiling meat.—Rules for knowing exactly the degrees of boiling.—Vegetables.—Remarks on making soup.—To clear soup.—Why it is not clear.—Coloring pot-au-feu.—Consommé.—*Crême de celeri*, a little known soup.—Recipes.. 65

Contents.

CHAPTER X.
SAUCES.

Remarks on making and flavoring sauces.—Espagnole or brown sauce as it should be.—How to make fine white sauce.. 70

CHAPTER XI.
WARMING OVER.

Remarks.—Salmi of cold meats.—Bœuf à la jardinière.—Bœuf au gratin.—Pseudo-beefsteak.—Cutlets à la jardinière.—Cromesquis of lamb.—Sauce piquant.—Miroton of beef.—Simple way of warming a joint.—Breakfast dish.—Stuffed beef.—Beef olives.—Chops à la poulette.—Devils.—Mephistophelian sauce.—Fritadella, twenty recipes in one.. 72

CHAPTER XII.
ON FRIANDISES.

Biscuit glacée at home (recipes).—Iced soufflés (recipes).—Baba and syrups for it (recipe).—Savarin and syrup (recipes).—Bouchées de dames.—How to make Curaçoa.—Maraschino.—Noyeau.. 84

CHAPTER XIII.
FRENCH CANDIES AT HOME.

How to make them.—Foudants.—Vanilla.—Almond cream.—Walnut cream.—Tutti frutti.—Various candies dipped in cream.—Chocolate creams.—Foudant panaché.—Punch drops... 91

CHAPTER XIV.
FOR PEOPLE OF VERY SMALL MEANS.

Remarks.—What may be made of a soup bone.—Several very economical dishes.—Pot roasts.—Dishes requiring no meat.. 96

CHAPTER XV.

A FEW THINGS IT IS WELL TO REMEMBER...................... 105

CHAPTER XVI.

ON SOME TABLE PREJUDICES................................ 108

CHAPTER XVII.

A CHAPTER OF ODDS AND ENDS.

Altering recipes.—How to have tarragon, burnet, etc.—Remarks on obtaining ingredients not in common use.—An impromptu salamander.—Larding needle.—How to have parsley fresh all winter without expense.—On having kitchen conveniences.—Anecdote related by Jules Gouffée.—On servants in America.—A little advice by way of valedictory 111

CONTENTS.

PART II.

CHAPTER XVIII.
	PAGE
Breakfast breads	119

CHAPTER XIX.
| Omelettes | 124 |

CHAPTER XX.
| General instructions | 126 |

CHAPTER XXI.
| Forcemeats—stuffing | 131 |

CHAPTER XXII.
| Vegetables | 134 |

CHAPTER XXIII.
| Soups | 140 |

CHAPTER XXIV.
| Fish | 150 |

CHAPTER XXV.
| Entrees | 157 |

CHAPTER XXVI.
| Roasts | 178 |

CHAPTER XXVII.
Poultry... 184

CHAPTER XXVIII.
Game... 191

CHAPTER XXIX.
Salads.. 196

CHAPTER XXX.
Boiled puddings of all kinds............................. 201

CHAPTER XXXI.
Pies, tarts and sweet omelettes.......................... 208

CHAPTER XXXII.
Dishes for cheese course, or supper...................... 216

CHAPTER XXXIII.
Sauces, savory and sweet................................. 219

CHAPTER XXXIV.
Cakes... 233

CATHERINE OWEN'S
NEW COOK BOOK.

PART I.
CULTURE AND COOKING.

CHAPTER I.

A FEW PRELIMINARY REMARKS.

ALEXANDRE DUMAS, *père*, after writing five hundred novels, says, "I wish to close my literary career with a book on cooking."

And in the hundred pages or so of preface—or perhaps overture would be the better word, since in it a group of literary men, while contributing recondite recipes, flourish trumpets in every key—to his huge volume he says, "I wish to be read by people of the world, and practiced by people of the art" (*gens de l'art*); and although *I* wish, like every one who writes, to be read by all the world, I wish to aid the practice, not of the professors of the culinary art, but those whose aspirations point to an enjoyment of the good things of life, but whose means of attaining them are limited.

There is a great deal of talk just now about cooking; in a lesser degree it takes its place as a popular topic with ceramics, modern antiques, and household art. The fact of it being in a mild way fashionable may do a little good to the eating world in general. And it may make it more easy to convince young women of refined proclivities that the art of cooking is not beneath their attention, to know that the Queen of England's daughters—and of course the cream of the London fair—have attended the lectures on the subject delivered at South Kensington, and that a young lady of rank, Sir James Coles's daughter, has been recording angel to the association, is in fact the R. C. C. who edits the "Official Handbook of Cookery."

But, notwithstanding all that has been done by South Kensington lectures in London and Miss Corson's Cooking School in New York to popularize the culinary art, one may go into a dozen houses, and find the ladies of the family with sticky fingers, scissors, and gum pot, busily porcelainizing clay jars, and not find one where they are as zealously trying to work out the problems of the "Official Handbook of Cookery."

I have nothing to say against the artistic distractions of the day. Anything that will induce love of the beautiful, and remove from us the possibility of a return to the horrors of hair-cloth and brocatel and crochet tidies, will be a stride in the right direction. But what I do protest against, is the fact, that the same refined girls and matrons, who so love to adorn their houses that they will spend hours improving a pickle jar, mediævalizing their furniture, or decorating the dinner service, will shirk everything that pertains to the preparation of food as dirty, disagreeable drudgery, and sit down to a commonplace, ill-prepared meal, served on those artistic plates, as complacently as if dainty food were not a refinement; as if heavy rolls and poor bread, burnt or greasy steak, and wilted potatoes did not smack of the shanty, just as loudly as coarse crockery or rag carpet—indeed far more so; the carpet and crockery may be due to poverty, but a dainty meal or its reverse will speak volumes for innate refinement or its lack in the woman who serves it. You see by my speaking of rag carpets and dainty meals in one breath, that I do not consider good things to be the privilege of the rich alone.

There are a great many dainty things the household of small or moderate means can have just as easily as the most wealthy. Beautiful bread—light, white, crisp—costs no more than the tough, thick-crusted boulder, with cavities like eye-sockets, that one so frequently meets with as *home-made bread*. As Hood says:

> " Who has not met with home-made bread,
> A heavy compound of putty and lead ?"

Delicious coffee is only a matter of care, not expense—and indeed in America the cause of poor food, even in a boarding-house, is seldom in the quality of the articles so much as in the preparation and selection of them—yet an epicure can breakfast well with fine bread and butter and good coffee. And this leads me to another thing : many people think that to give too much attention to food shows gluttony. I have heard a lady say with a tone of virtuous rebuke, when the conversation turned from fashions to cooking, " I give very little time to cooking, we eat to live only "—which is exactly what an animal does. Eating to live is mere feeding. Brillat-Savarin, an abstemious eater himself, among other witty things on the same topic says, "*L'animal se repait, l'homme mange, l'homme d'esprit seul sait manger.*"

Nine people out of ten, when they call a man an epicure, mean it as a sort of reproach, a man who is averse to every-day food, one whom plain fare would fail to satisfy ; but Grimod de la Reyniere, the most celebrated gourmet of his day, author of "*Almanach des Gourmands,*" and authority on all matters culinary of the last century, said, "A true epicure can dine well on one dish, provided it is excellent of its kind." Excellent, that is it. A little care will generally secure to us the refinement of having only on the table what is excellent of its kind. If it is but potatoes and salt, let the salt be ground fine, and the potatoes white and mealy. Thackeray says, an epicure is one who never tires of brown bread and fresh butter, and in this sense every New Yorker who has his rolls from the Brevoort House, and uses Darlington butter, is an epicure. There seems to me, more mere animalism in wading through a long bill of fare, eating three or four indifferently cooked vegetables, fish, meat, poultry, each second-rate in quality, or made so by bad cooking, and declaring that you have dined well, and are easy to please, than there is in taking pains to have a perfectly broiled chop, a fine potato, and a salad, on which any true epicure could dine well, while on the former fare he would leave the table hungry.

Spenser points a moral for me when he says, speaking of the Irish in 1580, "That wherever they found a plot of shamrocks or water-cresses they had a feast;" but there were gourmets even among them, for "some gobbled the green food as it came, and some picked the faultless stalks, and looked for the bloom on the leaf."

Thus it is, when I speak of "good living," I do not mean expensive living or high living, but living so that the table may be as elegant as the dishes on which it is served.

I believe there exists a feeling, not often expressed perhaps, but prevalent among young people, that for a lady to cook with her own hands is vulgar; to love to do it shows that she is of low intellectual caliber, a sort of drawing-room Bridget. When or how this idea arose it would be difficult to say, for in the middle ages cooks were often noble; a Montmorency was *chef de cuisine* to Philip of Valois; Montesquieu descended, and was not ashamed of his descent, from the second cook of the Connetable de Bourbon, who ennobled him. And from Lord Bacon, "brightest, greatest, meanest of mankind," who took, it is said, great interest in cooking, to Talleyrand, the Machiavelli of France, who spent an hour every day with his cook, we find great men delighting in the art as a recreation.

It is surprising that such an essentially artistic people as Americans should so neglect an art which a great French writer calls the "*science mignonne* of all distinguished men of the world." Napoleon the Great so fully recognized the social value of keeping a good table that, although no gourmet himself, he wished all his chief functionaries to be so. "Keep a good table," he told them; "if you get into debt for it I will pay." And later, one of his most devoted adherents, the Marquis de Cussy, out of favor with Louis XVIII. on account of that very devotion, found his reputation as a gourmet very serviceable to him. A friend applied for a place at court for him, which Louis refused, till he heard that M. de Cussy had invented the mixture of cream, strawberries, and champagne, when he granted the petition at once. Nor is this a solitary instance in history where culinary skill has been a passport to fortune to its possessor. Savarin relates that the Chevalier d'Aubigny, exiled from France, was in London, in utter poverty, notwithstanding which, by chance, he was invited to dine at a tavern frequented by the young bucks of that day.

After he had finished his dinner, a party of young gentlemen, who had been observing him from their table, sent one of their number with many apologies and excuses to beg of him, as a son of a nation renowned for their salads, to be kind enough to mix theirs for them. He complied, and while occupied in making the salad, told them frankly his story, and did not hide his poverty. One of the gentlemen, as they parted, slipped a five-pound note into his hand, and his need of it was so great that he did not obey the prompting of his pride, but accepted it.

A few days later he was sent for to a great house, and learned on his arrival that the young gentleman he had obliged at the tavern had spoken so highly of his salad that they begged him to do the same thing again. A very handsome sum was tendered him on his departure, and afterwards he had frequent calls on his skill, until it became the fashion to have salads prepared by d'Aubigny, who became a well-known character in London, and was called "*the fashionable salad-maker.*" In a few years he amassed a large fortune by this means, and was in such request that his carriage would drive from house to house, carrying him and his various condiments —for he took with him everything that could give variety to his concoctions—from one place, where his services were needed, to another.

The contempt for this art of cooking is confined to this country, and to the lower middle classes in England. By the "lower middle classes" I mean, what Carlyle terms the gigocracy—*i.e.*, people sufficiently well-to-do to keep a gig or phaeton—well-to-do tradesmen, small professional men, the class whose womenkind would call themselves "genteel," and many absurd stories are told of the determined ignorance and pretense of these would-be ladies. But in no class above this is a knowledge of cooking a thing to be ashamed of; in England, indeed, so far from that being the case, indifference to the subject, or lack of understanding and taste for certain dishes is looked upon as a sort of proof of want of breeding. Not to like curry, macaroni, or parmesan, *pâté de fois gras*, mushrooms, and such like, is a sign that you have not been all your life accustomed to good living. Mr. Hardy, in his "Pair of Blue Eyes," cleverly hits this prejudice when he makes Mr. Swancourt say, "I knew the fellow wasn't a gentleman; he had no acquired tastes, never took Worcestershire sauce."

Abroad many women of high rank and culture devote a good deal of time to a thorough understanding of the subject. We have a lady of the "lordly line of proud St. Clair" writing for us "Dainty Dishes," and doing it with a zest that shows she enjoys her work, although she does once in a while forget something she ought to have mentioned, and later still we have Miss Rose Coles writing the "Official Handbook of Cookery."

But it is in graceful, refined France that cookery is and has been, a pet art. Any bill of fare or French cookery book will betray to a thoughtful reader the attention given to the subject by the wittiest, gayest, and most beautiful women, and the greatest men. The high-sounding names attached to French standard dishes are no mere caprice or homage of a French cook to the great in the land, but actually point out their inventor. Thus *Bechamel* was invented by the Marquis de Bechamel, as a sauce for codfish; while *Filets de Lapereau à la*

Berry were invented by the Duchess de Berry, daughter of the regent Orleans, who himself invented *Pain à la d'Orleans*, while to Richelieu we are indebted for hundreds of dishes besides the renowned mayonnaise.

Cailles à la Mirepois, Chartreuse à la Mauconseil, Poulets à la Villeroy, betray the tastes of the three great ladies whose name they bear.

But not in courts alone has the art had its devotees. Almost every great name in French literature brings to mind something its owner said or did about cooking. Dumas, who was a prince of cooks, and of whom it is related that in 1860, when living at Varennes, St. Maur, dividing his time, as usual, between cooking and literature (*Lorsqu'il ne faisait pas sauter un roman, il faisait sauter des petits oignons*), on Mountjoye, a young artist friend and neighbor, going to see him, he cooked dinner for him. Going into the poultry yard, after donning a white apron, he wrung the neck of a chicken; then to the kitchen garden for vegetables, which he peeled and washed himself; lit the fire, got butter and flour ready, put on his saucepans, then cooked, stirred, tasted, seasoned until dinner time. Then he entered in triumph and announced, "*Le diner est servi.*" For six months he passed three or four days a week cooking for Mountjoye. This novelist's book says, in connection with the fact that great cooks in France have been men of literary culture, and literary men often fine cooks, "It is not surprising that literary men have always formed the *entourage* of a great chef, for, to appreciate thoroughly all there is in the culinary art, none are so well able as men of letters; accustomed as they are to all refinements, they can appreciate better than others those of the table," thus paying himself and confrères a delicate little compliment at the expense of the non-literary world; but, notwithstanding the naïve self-glorification, he states a fact that helps to point my moral, that indifference to cooking does not indicate refinement, intellect, or social pre-eminence.

Brillat-Savarin, grave judge as he was, and abstemious eater, yet has written the book of books on the art of eating. It was he who said, "Tell me what you eat, I will tell you what you are," as pregnant with truth as the better-known proverb it paraphrases.

Malherbe loved to watch his cook at work. I think it was he who said, "A coarse-minded man could never be a cook," and Charles Baudelaire, the Poe of France, takes a poet's view of our daily wants, when he says, "that an ideal cook must have a great deal of the poet's nature, combining something of the voluptuary with the man of science learned in the chemical principles of matter;" although he goes further than we care to follow when he says, that the question of sauces and seasoning requires "a chapter as grave as a *feuilleton de science.*"

It has been said by foreigners that Americans care nothing for the refinements of the table, but I think they do care. I have known many a woman in comfortable circumstances long to have a good table, many a man aspire to better things, and if he could only get them at home would pay any money. But the getting them at home is the difficulty; on a table covered with exquisite linen, glass, and silver, whose presiding queen is more likely than not a type of the American lady—graceful, refined, and witty—on such a table, with such surroundings, will come the plentiful, coarse, commonplace dinner.

The chief reason for this is lack of knowledge on the

part of our ladies: know how to do a thing yourself, and you will get it well done by others. But how are many of them to know? The daughters of the wealthy in this country often marry struggling men, and they know less about domestic economy than ladies of the higher ranks abroad; not because English or French ladies take more part in housekeeping, but because they are at home all their lives. Ladies of the highest rank never go to a boarding or any other school, and these are the women who, with some few exceptions, know best how things should be done. They are at home listening to criticisms from papa, who is an epicure perhaps, on the shortcomings of his own table, or his neighbors'; from mamma, as to what the soup lacks, why cook is not a "*cordon bleu*," etc., while our girls are at school, far away from domestic comments, deep in the agonies of algebra perhaps ; and directly they leave school, in many cases they marry. As a preparation for the state of matrimony most of them learn how to make cake and preserves, and the very excellence of their attainments in that way proves how easy it would be for them, with their dainty fingers and good taste, to far excel their European cousins in that art which a French writer says is based on "reason, health, common sense, and sound taste."

Here let me say, I do not by any means advocate a woman, who can afford to pay a first-rate cook, avoiding the expense by cooking herself ; on the contrary, I think no woman is justified in doing work herself that she has the means given her to get done by employing others. I have no praise for the economical woman, who, from a desire to save, does her own work *without necessity for economy.* It is *not* her work; the moment she can afford to employ others it is the work of some less fortunate person. But in this country, it often happens that a good cook is not to be found for money, although the raw material of which one might be made is much oftener at hand. And if ladies would only practice the culinary art with as much, nay, half as much assiduity as they give to a new pattern in crochet; devote as much time to attaining perfection in one dish or article of food, be it perfect bread, or some French dish which father, brother, or husband goes to Delmonico's to enjoy, as they do to the crochet tidies or embroidered rugs with which they decorate their drawing-rooms, they could then take the material, in the shape of any ambitious girl they may meet with, and make her a fine cook. In the time they take to make a dozen tidies, they would have a dozen dishes at their fingers' ends; and let me tell you, the woman who can cook a dozen things, outside of preserves, in a *perfect* manner is a rarity here, and a good cook anywhere, for, by the time the dozen are accomplished, she will have learned so much of the art of cooking that all else will come easy. One good soup, bouillon, and you have the foundation of all others; two good sauces, white sauce and brown, "*les sauces mères*" as the French call them (mothers of all other sauces), and all others are matters of detail. Learn to make one kind of roll perfectly, as light, plump, and crisp as Delmonico's, and all varieties are at your fingers' ends; you can have kringles, Vienna rolls, Kreuznach horns, Yorkshire tea cakes, English Sally Lunns and Bath buns; all are then as easy to make as common soda biscuit. In fact, in cooking, as in many other things, "*ce n'est que le premier pas que coûte;*" failures are almost certain at the beginning, but a failure is often a step toward success—if we only know the reason of the failure.

CHAPTER II.

ON BREAD.

OF all articles of food, bread is perhaps the one about which most has been written, most instruction given, and most failures made. Yet what adds more to the elegance of a table than exquisite bread or breads, and —unless you live in a large city and depend on the baker —what so rare? A lady who is very proud of her table, and justly so, said to me quite lately, "I cannot understand how it is we never have really fine home-made bread. I have tried many recipes, following them closely, and I can't achieve anything but a commonplace loaf with a thick, hard crust; and as for rolls, they are my despair. I have wasted eggs, butter, and patience so often that I have determined to give them up, but a fine loaf I will try for."

"And when you achieve the fine loaf, you may revel in home-made rolls," I answered.

And so I advise every one first to make perfect bread, light, white, crisp, and *thin-crusted*, that rarest thing in home-made bread.

I have read over many recipes for bread, and am convinced that when the time allowed for rising is specified, it is invariably too short. One standard book directs you to leave your sponge two hours, and the bread when made up a *quarter of an hour*. This recipe strictly followed must result in heavy, tough bread. As bread is so important, and so many fail, I will give my own method from beginning to end; not that there are not numberless good recipes, but simply because they frequently need adapting to circumstances, and altering a recipe is one of the things a tyro fears to do.

I make a sponge over night, using a dried yeast-cake soaked in a pint of warm water, to which I add a spoonful of salt, and, if the weather is warm, as much soda as will lie on a dime; make this into a stiff batter with flour—it may take a quart or less, flour varies so much, to give a rule is impossible; but if, after standing, the sponge has a watery appearance, make it thicker by sprinkling in more flour, beat hard a few minutes, and cover with a cloth—in winter keep a piece of thick flannel for the purpose, as a chill is fatal to your sponge—and set in a warm place free from draughts.

The next morning, when the sponge is quite light—that is to say, at least twice the bulk it was, and like a honeycomb—take two quarts of flour, more or less, as you require, but I recommend at first a small baking, and this will make three small loaves; in winter, flour should be dried and warmed; put it in your mixing bowl, and turn the sponge into a hole in the center. Have ready some water, rather more than lukewarm, but not *hot*. Add it gradually, stirring your flour into the sponge at the same time. The great fault in making bread is getting the dough too stiff; it should be as soft as possible, without being at all sticky or wet. Now knead it with both hands from all sides into the center; keep this motion, occasionally dipping your hands into the flour if the dough sticks, but do not add more flour unless the paste sticks very much; if you have the right consistency it will be a smooth mass, very soft to the touch, *yet not sticky*, but this may not be attained at a first mixing without adding flour by degrees. When you have kneaded the dough until it leaves the bowl all round, set it in a warm place to rise. When it is well risen, feels very soft and warm to the touch, and is twice its bulk, knead it once more thoroughly, then put it in tins either floured, and the flour not adhering shaken out, or buttered, putting in each a piece of dough half the size you intend your loaf to be. Now everything depends on your oven. Many people bake their bread slowly, leaving it in the oven a long time, and this causes a thick, hard crust. When baked in the modern iron oven, quick baking is necessary. Let the oven be quite hot, then put a little ball of paste in, and if it browns palely in seven to ten minutes it is about right; if it burns, it is too hot; open the damper ten minutes. Your bread, after it is in the tins, will rise much more quickly than the first time. Let it get light, but not too light—*twice its bulk* is a good rule; but if it is light before your oven is ready, and thus in danger of getting too porous, work it down with your hand, it will not harm it, although it is better so to manage that the oven waits for the bread rather than the bread for the oven. A small loaf—and by all means make them small until you have gained experience—will not take more than three quarters of an hour to bake; when a nice yellow brown, take it out, turn it out of the tin into a cloth, and tap the bottom; if it is crisp and smells cooked, the loaf is done. Once the bottom is brown it need remain no longer. Should that, however, from fault of your oven, be not brown, but soft and white, you must put it back in the oven, the bottom upwards. An oven that does not bake at the bottom will, however, be likely to spoil your bread. It is sometimes caused by a careless servant leaving a collection of ashes underneath it; satisfy yourself that all the flues are perfectly clean and clear before beginning to bake, and if it still refuses to do its duty, change it, for you will have nothing but loss and vexation of spirit while you have it in use. I think you will find this bread white, evenly porous (not with small holes in one part and caverns in another; if it is so you have made your dough too stiff, and it is not sufficiently kneaded), and with a thin, crisp crust. Bread will surely fail to rise at all if you have scalded the yeast; the water must never be too hot. In winter, if it gets chilled, it will only rise slowly, or not at all, and in using baker's or German yeast take care that it is not stale, which will cause heavy, irregular bread.

In making bread with compressed yeast proceed in exactly the same way, excepting that the sponge will not need to be set over night, unless you want to bake very early.

If you have once produced bread to your satisfaction you will find no difficulty in making rolls. Proceed as follows:

Take a piece of the dough from your baking after it has risen once. To a piece as large as a man's fist take a large tablespoonful of butter and a little powdered sugar; work them into the dough, put it in a bowl, cover it, and set it in a warm place to rise—a shelf behind the stove is best; if you make this at the same time as your bread, you will find it takes longer to rise; the butter causes that difference; when very light, much lighter than your bread should be, take your hand and push it down till it is not larger than when you put it in the bowl; let it rise again, and again push it down, but not so thoroughly; do this once or twice more, and you have the secret of light rolls. You will find them rise very quickly, after once or twice pushing down. When they have risen the third or fourth time, take a little butter on your hands, and break off small pieces about the size of a walnut and roll them round. Either put them on a tin close together, to be broken apart, or an inch or two from each other, in which case work in a little more flour, and cut a cleft on the top, and once more set to rise; half an hour will be long enough generally, but in this case you must judge for yourself, they sometimes take an hour; if they look swelled very much and smooth they will be ready. Have a nice hot oven, and bake for twelve to fifteen minutes.

Add a little more sugar to your dough and an egg, go through the same process, brush them over with sugar dissolved in milk, and you will have delicious rusks.

The above is my own method of making rolls, and the simplest I know of; but there are numbers of other recipes given in cookery books which would be just as good if the exact directions for letting them rise were given. As a test—and every experiment you try will be so much gained in your experience—follow the recipe given for rolls in any good cookery book, take part of the dough and let it rise as therein directed, and bake, set the other part to rise as *I* direct, and notice the difference.

KREUZNACH HORNS.—Either take a third of the dough made for bread with three quarts of flour, or set a sponge with a pint of flour and a yeast-cake soaked in half a pint of warm water or milk, making it into a stiffish dough with another pint of flour; then add four ounces of butter, a *little* sugar, and two eggs; work well.

If you use the bread dough, you will need to dredge in a little more flour on account of the eggs, but not *very much;* then set to rise as for rolls, work it down twice or thrice, then turn the dough out on the molding board lightly floured, roll it as you would pie-crust into pieces six inches square, and quarter of an inch thick, make two sharp, quick cuts across it from corner to corner, and you will have from each square four three-cornered pieces of paste; spread each *thinly* with soft butter, flour lightly, and roll up very lightly from the wide side, taking care that it is not squeezed together in any way; lay them on a tin with the side on which the point comes uppermost, and bend round in the form of a horseshoe; these will take some time to rise; when they have swollen much and look light, brush them over with white of egg (not beaten) or milk and butter, and bake in a good oven.

KRINGLES are made from the same recipe, but with another egg and two ounces of sugar (powdered) added to the dough when first set to rise; then, when well risen two or three times, instead of rolling with a pin as for horns, break off pieces, roll between your hands as thick as your finger, and form into figure eights, rings, fingers; or take three strips, flour and roll them as thick as your finger, tapering at each end; lay them on the board, fasten the three together at one end, and then lay one over the other in a plait, fasten the other end, and set to rise, bake; when done, brush over with sugar dissolved in milk, and sprinkle with sugar.

All these breads are delicious for breakfast, and may easily be had without excessive early rising if the sponge is set in the *morning,* dough made in the afternoon, and the rising and working done in the evening; when, instead of making up into rolls, horns, or kringles, push the dough down thoroughly, cover with a damp folded cloth, and put in a *very* cold place if in summer—not on ice of course—then next morning, as soon as the fire is alight, mold, but do not push down any more, put in a very warm spot, and when light, bake.

In summer, as I have said, I think it safest, to prevent danger of souring, to put a little soda in the sponge for bread; and for rolls, or anything requiring to rise several times, it is an essential precaution.

BRIOCHE.—I suppose the very name of this delectable French dainty will call up in the mind's eye of many who read this book that great "little" shop, *Au Grand Brioche,* on the Boulevarde Poissonière, where, on Sunday afternoons, scores of boys from the Lycées form *en queue* with the general public, waiting the hour when the piles of golden brioche shall be ready to exchange for their eager sous. But I venture to say, a really fine brioche is rarely eaten on this side the Atlantic. They being a luxury welcome to all, and especially aromatic of Paris, I tried many times to make them, obtaining for that purpose recipes from French friends, and from standard French books, but never succeeded in producing the ideal brioche until I met with Gouffé's great book, the *"Livre de Cuisine,"* after reading which, I may here say, all secrets of the French kitchen are laid bare; no effort is spared to make everything plain, from the humble *pot-au-feu* to the most gorgeous monumental *plât.* And I would refer any one who wants to become proficient in any French dish, to that book, feeling sure that, in following strictly the directions, there will be no failure. It is the one book I have met with on the subject in which no margin is left for your own knowledge, if you have it, to fill up. But to the brioche.

PARIS JOCKEY-CLUB RECIPE FOR BRIOCHE.

Sift one pound of flour, take one fourth of it, and add rather more than half a cake of compressed yeast, dissolved in half a gill of warm water, make into a sponge with a *very little* more water, put it in a warm place; when it is double its volume take the rest of the flour, make a hole in the center, and put in it an equal quantity of salt and sugar, about a teaspoonful, and two tablespoonfuls of water to dissolve them. Three quarters of a pound of butter and four eggs, beat well, then add another egg, beat again, and add another, and so on until seven have been used; the paste must be soft, but not spread; if too firm, add another egg. Now mix this paste with the sponge thoroughly, beating until the paste leaves the sides of the bowl, then put it in a crock and cover; let it stand four hours in a warm place, then turn it out on a board, *spread it and double it four times*, return it to the crock, and let it rise again two hours; repeat the former process of doubling and spreading, and put it in a very cold place for two hours, or until you want to use it. Mold in any form you like, but the true brioche is two pieces, one as large again as the other; form the large one into a ball, make a deep depression in the center, on which place the smaller ball, pressing it gently in; cut two or three gashes round it with a sharp knife, and bake a beautiful golden brown. These brioche are such a luxury, and so sure to come out right, that the trouble of making them is well worth the taking, and for another reason: every one knows the great difficulty of making puff paste in summer, and a short paste is never handsome; but take a piece of brioche paste, roll it out thin, dredge with flour, fold and roll again, then use as you would puff paste; if for sweet pastry, a little powdered sugar may be sprinkled through it instead of dredging with flour. This makes a very handsome and delicious crust. Or, another use to which it may be put is to roll it out, cut it in rounds, lay on them mince-meat, orange marmalade, jam, or merely sprinkle with currants, chopped citron, and spices, fold, press the edges, and bake.

Before quitting the subject of breads I must introduce a novelty which I will call "soufflée bread." It is quickly made, possible even when the fire is poor, and so delicious that I know you will thank me for making you acquainted with it.

Use two or three eggs according to size you wish, and to each egg a tablespoonful of flour. Mix the yolks with the flour and with them a dessert-spoonful of butter melted, and enough milk to make a very *thick* batter, work, add a pinch of salt and a teaspoonful of sugar, work till quite smooth, then add the whites of the eggs in a firm froth, stir them in gently, and add a *quarter* teaspoonful of soda and half a one of cream of tartar. Have ready an iron frying-pan (or an earthen one that will stand heat is better), made hot with a tablespoonful of butter in it, also hot, but not so hot as for frying. Pour the batter (which should be of the consistency of sponge cake batter) into the pan, cover it with a lid or tin plate, and set it back of the stove if the fire is hot—if very slow it may be forward; when well risen and near done, put it in the oven, or if the oven is cold you may turn it gently, not to deaden it. Serve when done (try with a twig), the under side uppermost; it should be of a fine golden brown and look like an omelet. This soufflée bread is equally good *baked* in a tin in which is rather more butter than enough to grease it; the oven must be *very hot indeed*. Cover it for the few minutes with a tin plate or lid, to prevent it scorching before it has risen; when it has puffed up remove the lid, and allow it to brown, ten to fifteen minutes should bake it; turn it out as you would sponge cake—very carefully, not to deaden it. To succeed with bread you must use the very best flour.

CHAPTER III.

PASTRY.

To MAKE good puff paste is a thing many ladies are anxious to do, and in which they generally fail, and this not so much because they do not make it properly, as because they handle it badly. A lady who was very anxious to excel in pastry once asked me to allow her to watch me make paste. I did so, and explained that there was more in the manner of using than in the making up. I then gave her a piece of my paste when completed, and asked her to cover some patty pans while I covered others, cautioning her as to the way she must cover them; yet, when those covered by her came out of the oven they had not risen at all, they were like rich short paste; while my own, made from the same paste, were toppling over with lightness. I had, without saying anything, pressed my thumb slightly on one spot of one of mine; in that spot the paste had not risen at all, and I think this practical demonstration of what I had tried to explain was more useful than an hour's talk would have been.

I will first give my method of making, which is the usual French way of making "*feuilletonage.*" Take one pound of butter, or half of it lard; press all the water out by squeezing it in a cloth; this is important, as the liquid in it would wet your paste; take a third of the butter, or butter and lard, and rub it into one pound of *fine* flour; add no salt if your butter is salted; then take enough water (to which you may add the well-beaten white of an egg, but it is not absolutely necessary) to make the flour into a smooth, firm dough; it must not be too stiff, or it will be hard to roll out, or too soft, or it will never make good paste; it should roll easily, yet not stick; work it till it is very smooth, then roll it out till it is half an inch thick; now lay the whole of the butter in the center, fold one-third the paste over, then the other third; it is now folded in three, with the butter completely hidden; now turn the ends toward you, and roll it till it is half an inch thick, taking care, by rolling very evenly, that the butter is not pressed out at the other end; now you have a piece of paste about two feet long, and not half that width; flour it lightly, and fold *over* one third and under one third, which will almost bring it to a square again; turn it round so that what was the side is now the end, and roll. Most likely now the butter will begin to break through, in which case fold it, after flouring lightly, in three, as before, and put it on a dish on the ice, covering it with a damp cloth. You may now either leave it for an hour or two, or till next day. Paste made the day before it is used is much better and easier to manage, and in winter it may be kept for four or five days in a cold place, using from it as required.

When ready to use your paste finish the making by rolling it out, dredging a *little* flour, and doubling it in three as before, and roll it out thin; do this until from first to last it has been so doubled and rolled seven times.

Great cooks differ on one or two points in making pastry; for instance, Soyer directs you to put the yolk of an egg instead of the white, and a squeeze of lemon juice into the flour, and expressly forbids you to work it before adding the mass of butter, while Jules Gouffé says, "work it until smooth and shining." I cannot pretend to decide between these differing doctors, but I pursue the method I have given and always have light pastry. And now to the handling of it : It must only be touched by the lightest fingers, every cut must be made with a sharp knife, and done with one quick stroke so that the paste is not dragged at all ; in covering a pie dish or patty pan, you are commonly directed to mold the paste over it as thin as possible, which conveys the idea that the paste is to be pressed over and so made thin ; this would destroy the finest paste in the world ; roll it thin, say for small tartlets, less than a quarter of an inch thick, for a pie a trifle thicker, then lay the dish or tin to be covered on the paste, and cut out with a knife, dipped in *hot* water or flour, a piece a little larger than the mold, then line with the piece you have cut, touching it as little as possible ; press only enough to make the paste adhere to the bottom, but on no account press the border; to test the necessity of avoiding this, gently press one spot on a tart, before putting it in the oven, only so much as many people always do in making pie, and watch the result. When your tartlets or pies are made, take each up on your left hand, and with a sharp knife dipped in flour trim it round quickly. To make the cover of a pie adhere to the under crust, lay the forefinger of your right hand lengthwise round the border, but as far from the edge as you can, thus forming a groove for the syrups, and pressing the cover on at the same time. A word here about fruit pies : Pile the fruit high in the center, leaving a space all round the sides almost bare of fruit, when the cover is on press gently the paste, as I have explained, into this groove, then make two or three deep holes in the groove; the juice will boil out of these holes and run round this groove, instead of boiling out through the edges and wasting.

This is the pastry-cook's way of making pies, and makes a much handsomer one than the usual flat method, besides saving your syrup. To ornament fruit pies or tartlets, whip the white of an egg, and stir in as much powdered sugar as will make a thin meringue—a large tablespoonful is usually enough—then when your pies or tartlets are baked, take them from the oven, glaze with the egg and sugar, and return to the oven, leaving the door open; when it has set into a frosty icing they are ready to serve.

It is worth while to accomplish puff paste, for so many dainty trifles may be made with it, which, attempted with the ordinary short paste, would be unsightly. Some of these that seem to me novel I will describe.

Rissolettes are made with trimmings of puff paste; if you have about a quarter of a pound left, roll it out very thin, about as thick as a fifty-cent piece; put about half a spoonful of marmalade or jam on it, in places about an inch apart, wet lightly round each, and place a piece of paste over all; take a small round cutter as large as a dollar, and press round the part where the marmalade or jam is with the thick part of the cutter; then cut them out with a cutter a size larger, lay them on a baking tin, brush over with white of egg; then cut some little rings the size of a quarter dollar, put one on each, egg over again, and bake twenty minutes in a nice hot oven; then sift white sugar all over, put them back in the oven to glaze; a little red currant jelly in each ring looks pretty; serve in the form of a pyramid.

PASTRY TABLETS.—Cut strips of paste three inches and a half long, and an inch and a half wide, and as thick as a twenty-five cent piece; lay on half of them a thin filmy layer of jam or marmalade, not jelly; then on each lay a strip without jam, and bake in a quick oven. When the paste is well risen and brown, take them out, glaze them with white of egg and sugar, and sprinkle chopped almonds over them; return to the oven till the glazing is set and the almonds just colored; serve them hot or cold on a napkin piled log-cabin fashion.

FRANGIPANÉ TARTLETS.—One quarter pint of cream, four yolks of eggs, two ounces of flour, three macaroons, four tablespoonfuls of powdered sugar, the peel of a grated lemon, and a little citron cut very fine, a little brandy and orange-flower water. Put all the ingredients, except the eggs, in a saucepan—of course you will mix the flour smooth in the cream first—let them come to a boil slowly, stirring to prevent lumps; when the flour smells cooked, take it off the fire for a minute, then stir the beaten yolks of eggs into it. Stand the saucepan in another of boiling water and return to the stove, stirring till the eggs seem done—about five minutes, if the water boils all the time. Line patty pans with puff paste, and fill with frangipane and bake. Ornament with chopped almonds and meringue, or not, as you please.

It is very difficult to make fine puff paste in warm weather, and almost impossible without ice; for this reason I think the brioche paste preferable; but if it is necessary to have it for any purpose, you must take the following precautions:

Have your water iced; have your butter as firm as

possible by being kept on ice till the last moment; make the paste in the coolest place you have, and under the breeze of an open window, if possible; make it the day before you use it, and put it on the ice between every "turn," as each rolling out is technically called; then leave it on the ice, as you use it, taking pieces from it as you need them, so that the warmth cannot soften the whole at once, when it would become quite unmanageable. The condition of the oven is a very important matter, and I cannot do better than transcribe the rules given by Gouffé, by which you may test its fitness for any purpose:

Put half a sheet of writing paper in the oven; if it catches fire it is too hot; open the dampers and wait ten minutes, when put in another piece of paper; if it blackens it is still too hot. Ten minutes later put in a third piece; if it gets *dark brown* the oven is right for all small pastry. Called *"dark brown paper heat." Light brown paper heat* is suitable for *vol-au-vents* or fruit pies. *Dark yellow paper heat* for large pieces of pastry or meat pies, pound cake, bread, etc. *Light yellow paper heat* for sponge cake, meringues, etc.

To obtain these various degrees of heat, you try paper every ten minutes till the heat required for your purpose is attained. But remember that "light yellow" means the paper only tinged; "dark yellow," the paper the color of ordinary pine wood; "light brown" is only a shade darker, about the color of nice pie-crust, and dark brown a shade darker, by no means coffee color.

CHAPTER IV.

WHAT TO HAVE IN YOUR STORE-ROOM.

One great trouble with many young housekeepers is betrayed by the common remark, " Cookery books always require so many things that one never has in the house, and they coolly order you to 'moisten with gravy,' 'take a little gravy,' as if you had only to go to the pump and get it." It is very true that economy in cooking is much aided by having a supply of various condiments; warmed-over meat may then be converted into a delicious little entrée with little trouble. I would recommend, therefore, any one who is in earnest about reforming her dinner table to begin by expending a few dollars in the following articles:

1 bottle of capers,	1 bottle of claret,
1 " olives,	1 " white wine,
1 " gherkins,	1 " sherry for cooking,
1 " soy,	1 " brandy,
1 " anchovies,	1 " Harvey sauce,
1 " tarragon vinegar,	1 " walnut ketchup.

And a package of compressed vegetables and a few bay leaves.

Ten dollars thus spent may seem a good deal of money to a young housewife trying to make her husband's salary go as far as it will; but I assure her it is in the end an economy, especially in a small family, who are so apt to get tired of seeing the same thing, that it has to be thrown or given away. With these condiments and others I have yet to mention you will have no trouble in using every scrap; not using it and eating it from a sense of duty, and wishing it was something better, but enjoying it. With your store-room well provided, you can indeed go for gravy "as if to the pump."

Besides the foregoing list of articles to be bought of any good grocer, there are others which can be made at home to advantage, and once made are always ready. Mushroom powder I prefer for any use to mushroom catsup; it is easily made and its uses are infinite. Sprinkled over steak (when it must be sifted) or chops, it is delicious. For ordinary purposes, such as flavoring soup or gravy, it need not be sifted. To prepare it, take a peck of large and very fresh mushrooms, look them over carefully that they are not wormy, then cleanse them with a piece of flannel from sand or grit, then peel them and put them in the sun or a cool oven to dry; they require long, slow drying, and must become in a state to crumble. Your peck will have diminished by the process into half a pint or less of mushroom powder, but you have the means with it of making a rich gravy at a few minutes' notice.

Apropos of gravies—that much-vexed question in small households—for without gravies on hand you cannot make good hash, or many other things that are miserable without, and excellent with it. Yet how difficult it is to have gravy always on hand every mistress of a small family knows, in spite of the constant advice to "save your trimming to make stock." Do by all means save your bones, gristle, odds and ends of meat of all kinds, and convert them into broth; but even if you do, it often happens that the days you have done so no gravy is required, and then it sours quickly in summer, although it may be arrested by reboiling. In no family of three or four are there odds and ends enough, unless there is a very extravagant table kept, to insure stock for every day. My remedy for this, then, is to make a stock that will keep for months or years—in other words, *glaze*. So very rarely forming part of a housewife's stores, yet so valuable that the fact is simply astonishing; with a piece of glaze, you have a dish of soup on an emergency, rich gravy for any purpose, and all with the expenditure of less time than would make a pot of sweetmeats.

Take six pounds of a knuckle of veal or leg of beef, cut it in pieces the size of an egg, as also half a pound of lean ham; then rub a quarter of a pound of butter on the bottom of your pot, which should hold two gallons; then put in the meat with half a pint of water, three middle-sized onions, with two cloves in each, a turnip, a carrot, and a *small* head of celery; then place over a quick fire, occasionally stirring it round, until the bottom of the pot is covered with a thick glaze, which will adhere lightly to the spoon; then fill up the pot with cold water, and when on the boiling point, draw it to the back of the stove, where it may gently simmer three hours, if veal, six if beef, carefully skimming it to remove scum. This stock, as it is, will make a delicious foundation, with the addition of salt, for all kinds of clear soup or gravies. To reduce it to glaze proceed as follows: Pass the stock through a fine hair sieve or cloth into a pan; then fill up the pot again with *hot* water, and let it boil four hours longer to obtain all the glutinous part from the meat; strain, and pour both stocks in a large pot or stew-pan together; set it over the fire, and let it boil as fast as possible with the lid off, leaving a large spoon in it to prevent it boiling over, and to stir occasionally. When reduced to about three pints, pour it into a small stew-pan or saucepan, set again to boil, but more slowly, skimming it if necessary; when it is reduced to a quart, set it where it will again boil quickly, stirring it well with a wooden spoon until it begins to get thick and of a fine yellowish-brown color; at this point be careful it does not burn.

You may either pour it into a pot for use, or, what is more convenient for making gravies, get a sausage skin from your butcher, cut a yard of it, tie one end very tightly, then pour into it by means of a large funnel the glaze; from this cut slices for use. A thick slice dissolved in hot water makes a cup of nutritious soup, into which you may put any cooked vegetables, or rice, or barley. A piece is very useful to take on a journey, especially for an invalid who does not want to depend on wayside hotel food, or is tired of beef-tea.

The foregoing is the orthodox recipe for glaze, and if you have to buy meat for the purpose the very best way in which you can make it; but if it happen that you have some strong meat soup or jelly, for which you have no use while fresh, then boil it down till it is thick and brown (not burnt); it will be excellent glaze; not so fine in flavor, perhaps, but it preserves to good use what would otherwise be lost. Very many people do not know the value of pork for making jelly. If you live in the country and kill a pig, use his hocks for making glaze instead of beef.

Glaze also adds much to the beauty of many dishes. If roast beef is not quite brown enough on any one spot set your jar of glaze—for this purpose it is well to have some put in a jar as well as in the skin—in boiling water. Keep a small stiff brush; such as are sold for the purpose at house-furnishing stores, called a glazing brush, are best; but you may manage with any other or even a stiff feather. When the glaze softens, as glue would do, brush over your meat with it, it will give the lacking brown; or, if you have a ham or tongue you wish to decorate you may "varnish" it, as it were, with the melted glaze; then when cold beat some fresh butter to a white cream, and with a kitchen syringe, if you have one, a stiff paper funnel if you have not, trace any design you please on the glazed surface; this makes a very handsome dish, and if your ham has been properly boiled will be very satisfactory to the palate. Of the boiling of ham I will speak in another chapter.

I have a few more articles to recommend for your store-room, and then I think you will find yourself equal to the emergency of providing an elegant little meal if called upon unexpectedly, provided you have any cold scraps at all in the house, and *maître d'hôtel* butter.

To make the latter, take half a pound of fine butter, one tablespoonful of very fresh parsley, chopped not too fine, salt, pepper, and a small tablespoonful of lemon juice; mix together, but do not work more than sufficient for that purpose, and pack in a jar, keeping it in a cool place. A tablespoonful of this laid in a hot dish on which you serve beefsteak, chops, or any kind of fish, is a great addition, and turns plain boiled potatoes into *pomme de terre à la maître d'hôtel.* It is excellent with stewed potatoes, or added to anything for which parsley is needed, and not always at hand; a spoonful with half the quantity of flour stirred into a gill of milk or water makes the renowned *maître d'hôtel* sauce (or English parsley butter) for boiled fish, mutton, or veal. In short, it is one of the most valuable things to have in the house. Equally valuable, even, and more elegant is the preparation known as "Ravigotte" or Montpellier butter.

Take one pound in equal quantities of chervil, tarragon, burnet (pimpernel), chives, and garden cress (peppergrass); scald *two* minutes, drain quite dry; pound in a mortar three hard eggs, three anchovies, and one scant ounce of pickled cucumbers, and same quantity of capers well pressed to extract the vinegar; add salt, pepper, and a bit of garlic half as large as a pea, rub all through a sieve; then put a pound of fine butter into the mortar, which must be well cleansed from the herbs, add the herbs, with two tablespoonfuls of oil and one of tarragon vinegar, mix perfectly, and if not of a fine green, add the juice of some pounded spinach.

This is the celebrated *"beurre de Montpellier,"* sold in Paris in tiny jars at a high price. Ravigotte is the same thing, only in place of the eggs, anchovies, pickles, and capers, put half a pound more butter; it is good, but less piquant.

Pack in a jar, and keep cool. This butter is excellent for many purposes. For salad, beaten with oil, vinegar, and yolks of eggs, as for mayonnaise, it makes a delicious dressing. For cold meat or fish it is excellent, and also for chops.

Two or three other articles serve to simplify the art of cooking in its especially difficult branches, and in the branches a lady finds difficult to attend to herself without remaining in the kitchen until the last minute before dinner; but with the aid of blanc and roux a fairly intelligent girl can make excellent sauces.

For roux melt slowly half a pound of butter over the fire, skim it, let it settle, then dredge in eight ounces of fine flour, stir it till it is of a bright brown, then put away in a jar for use.

Blanc is the same thing, only it is not allowed to brown; it should be stirred only enough to make all hot through, then put away in a jar.

If you need thickening for a white sauce and do not wish to stand over it yourself, having taught your cook the simple fact that a piece of blanc put into the milk *before it boils* (or it will harden instead of melt) and allowed to dissolve, stirring constantly, will make the sauce you wish, she will be able at all times to produce a white sauce that you need not be ashamed of. When the sauce is nearly ready to serve, stir in a good piece of butter—a large spoonful to half a pint; when mixed, the sauce is ready. Brown sauce can always be made by taking a cup of broth or soup and dissolving in the same way a piece of the roux; and also, if desired, a piece of Montpellier butter. If there is no soup of course you make it with a piece of glaze.

Brown flour is also a convenient thing to have ready; it is simply cooking flour in the oven until it is a *pale* brown; if it is allowed to get dark it will be bitter, and, that it may brown evenly, it requires to be laid on a large flat baking pan and stirred often. Useful for thickening stews, hash, etc.

CHAPTER V.

LUNCHEON.

LUNCHEON is usually, in this country, either a forlorn meal of cold meat or hash, or else a sort of early dinner, both of which are a mistake. If it is veritably *luncheon*, and not early dinner, it should be as unlike that later meal as possible for variety's sake, and, in any but very small families, there are so many dishes more suitable for luncheon than any other meal, that it is easy to have great variety with very little trouble.

I wish it were more the fashion here to have many of the cold dishes which are popular on the other side the Atlantic; and, in spite of the fact that table prejudices are very difficult to get over, I will append a few recipes in the hope that some lady, more progressive than prejudiced, may give them a trial, convinced that their excellence, appearance, and convenience will win them favor.

By having most dishes cold at luncheon, it makes it a distinct meal from the hot breakfast and dinner. In summer, the cold food and a salad is especially refreshing; in winter, a nice hot soup or purée—thick soup is preferable at luncheon to clear, which is well fitted to precede a heavy meal—and some savory *entrée* are very desirable, while cold raised pie, galantine, jellied fish, and potted meats may ever, at that season, find their appropriate place on the luncheon table. The potatoes, which are the only vegetable introduced at strict lunch, should be prepared in some fancy manner, as croquettes, mashed and browned, *à la mâitre d'hôtel*, or in snow. The latter mode is pretty and novel; I will, therefore, include it in my recipes for luncheon dishes. Omelets, too, are excellent at luncheon.

In these remarks I am thinking especially of large families, whose luncheon table might be provided with a dish of galantine, one of collared fish, and a meat pie, besides the steak, cutlets, or warmed-over meat, without anything going to waste. In winter most cold jellied articles will keep a fortnight, and in summer three or four days.

WINDSOR PIE.—Take slices of veal cutlet, half an inch thick, and very thin slices of lean boiled ham; put at the bottom of one of these veal-pie dishes or "bakers," about two to three inches deep, a layer of the veal, seasoned, then one of ham, then one of force-meat, made as follows: Take a little veal, or if you have sausage-meat ready-made, it will do, as much fine dry bread-crumbs, a dessert-spoonful of *finely* chopped parsley, in which is a salt-spoonful of powdered thyme, savory, and marjoram, if you have them, with salt and pepper, and mix with enough butter to make it a crumbling paste; lay a *thin* layer of this on the ham, then another of veal, then ham and force-meat again, until the dish is quite full. Lay something flat upon it, and then a weight for an hour. You must have prepared, from bones and scraps of veal, about a pint of stiff veal jelly; pour this over the meat, and then take strips of rich puff paste (the *brioche* paste would be excellent in hot weather), wet the edge of the dish, and lay the strips round, pressing them lightly to the dish; roll the cover a little larger than the top of the dish, and lay it on, first wetting the surface, *not the edge*, of the strips round the lips of the dish; press the two together, then make a hole in the center and ornament as you please; but I never ornament the *edge* of a pie, as it is apt to prevent the paste from rising. An appropriate and simple ornament for meat pies is to roll a piece of paste very thin, cut it in four diamond-shaped pieces, put one point of each to the hole in the center so that you have one on each end, and one each side, then roll another little piece of paste as thin as possible, flour it and double it, then double it again, bring all the corners together in your hand, like a little bundle, then with a sharp knife give a quick cut over the top of the ball of paste, cutting quite deeply, then another across; if your cut has been clean and quick, you will now be able to turn half back the leaves of paste as if it were a half-blown rose. The ends which you have gathered together in your hand are to be inserted in the hole in the center of the pie. Then brush over with yolk of egg beaten very well in a little milk or water, and bake an hour and a half.

This way of covering and ornamenting a pie is appropriate for all meat pies; pigeon pie should, however, have the little red feet skinned by dipping in boiling water, then rubbed in a cloth, when skin and nails peel off; if allowed to lie in the water, the flesh comes too; then one pair is put at each end of the pie, a hole being cut to insert them, or four are put in the center instead of the rose.

The Windsor pie is intended to be eaten cold, as are all veal and ham pies, the beauty of the jelly being lost in a hot pie. Do not fail to try it on that account, for cold pies are excellent things.

ANOTHER VEAL AND HAM PIE, more usual, and probably the "weal and hammer" that "mellered the organ" of Silas Wegg, was manufactured by Mrs. Boffin from this recipe; it is as follows:

Take the thick part of breast of veal, removing all the bones, which put on for gravy, stewing them long and slowly; put a layer of veal, pepper and salt, then a thin sprinkling of ham; if boiled, cut in slices; if raw, cut a slice in dice, which scald before using, then more veal and again ham. If force-meat balls are liked, make some force-meat as for Windsor pie, using if you prefer it chopped hard-boiled eggs in place of chopped meat, and binding into a paste with a raw egg; then make into balls, which drop into the crevices of the pie; boil two or three eggs quite hard, cut each in four and lay them round the sides and over the top, pour in about a gill of gravy, and cover the same as the Windsor pie. In either of these pies the force-meat may be left out, a sweetbread cut up, or mushroons put in.

A chicken pie to eat cold is very fine made in this way.

RAISED PORK PIES are so familiar to every one who has visited England, and, in spite of the greasy idea, are so very good, that I introduce a well-tried recipe, feeling sure any one who eats pork at all will find it worth while to give them a trial; they will follow it with many another.

The paste for them is made as follows:

Rub into two pounds of flour a liberal half pound of butter, then melt in half a pint of hot, but not boiling milk, another half pound—or it may be lard; pour this into the flour, and knead it into a smooth, firm paste. Properly raised pies should be molded by hand, and I will endeavor to describe the method in case any persevering lady would like to try and have the orthodox thing.

But pie molds of tin, opening at the side, are to be bought, and save much trouble; the mold, if used, should be well buttered, and the pie taken out when done, and returned to the oven for the sides to brown.

To "raise" a pie, proceed thus: While the paste is warm, form a ball of paste into a cone; then with the fist work inside it, till it forms an oval cup; continue to knead till you have the walls of an even thickness, then pinch a fold all around the bottom. If properly done, you have an oval, flat-bottomed crust, with sides about two inches high; fill this with pork, fat and lean together, well peppered and salted; then work an oval cover, as near the size of the bottom cover as you can, and wet the edges of the wall, lay the cover on, and pinch to match the bottom; ornament as directed for Windsor pie, wash with egg, and bake a pale brown in a moderate oven; they must be well cooked, or the meat will not be good. One containing a pound of meat may be cooked an hour and a quarter. All these pies are served in slices, cut through to the bottom.

Galantines are very handsome dishes, not very difficult to make, and generally popular. I give a recipe for a very simple and delicious one:

Take a fine breast of veal, remove all gristle, tendons, bones, and trim to fifteen inches in length and eight wide; use the trimmings and bones to help make the jelly, then put on the meat a layer of force-meat made thus: Take one pound of sausage meat, or lean veal, to which add half a pound of bread-crumbs, parsley and thyme to taste; grate a *little* nutmeg, pepper, salt, and the juice of half a lemon; have also some long strips an inch thick of fat bacon or pork, and lean of veal, and lean ham, well seasoned with pepper, salt, and finely chopped shallots. Lay on the meat a layer of force-meat an inch thick, leaving an inch and a half on each side uncovered; then lay on your strips of ham, veal, and bacon fat, alternately; then another of force-meat, but only half an inch thick, as too much force-meat will spoil the appearance of the dish; if you have any cold tongue, lay some strips in, also a few blanched pistachio nuts (to be obtained of a confectioner) will give the appearance of true French galantine. Roll up the veal, and sew it with a packing or coarse needle and fine twine, tie it firmly up in a piece of linen. Observe that you do not put your pistachio nuts amid the force-meat, where, being green, their appearance would be lost; put them in crevices of the meats.

Cook this in sufficient water to cover, in which you must have the trimmings of the breast and a knuckle of veal, or hock of pork, two onions, a carrot, half a head of celery, two cloves, a blade of mace, and a good bunch of parsley, thyme and bay leaf, two ounces of salt. Set the pot on the fire till it is at boiling point, then draw it to the back and let it simmer three hours, skimming carefully; then take it from the fire, leaving it in the stock till nearly cold; then take it out, remove the string from the napkin, and roll the galantine up tighter—if too tight at first it will be hard—tying the napkin at each end only; then place it on a dish, set another dish on it, on which place a fourteen-pound weight; this will cause it to cut firm. When quite cold, remove strings and cloth, and it is ready to be ornamented with jelly. When the stock in which the galantine was cooked is cold take off the fat and clarify it, first trying, however, if it is in right condition, by putting a little on ice. If it is not stiff enough to cut firm, you must reduce it by boiling; if too stiff, that is approaching glaze, add a *little* water, then clarify by adding whites of eggs, as directed to clarify soup (see soups). A glass of sherry and two spoonfuls of tarragon or common vinegar are a great improvement. Some people like this jelly cut in dice, to ornament the galantine, part of it may then also serve to ornament other dishes at the table. But I prefer to have the galantine enveloped in jelly, which may be done by putting it in an oblong soup tureen or other vessel that will contain it, leaving an inch space all round, then pouring the jelly over it.

Jellied fish is a favorite dish with many, and is very simple to prepare; it is also very ornamental. Take flounders or almost any flat fish that is cheapest at the time you require them. Clean and scrape them, cut them in small pieces, but do not cut off the fins; put them in a stew-pan with a few small button onions or one large one, a half teaspoonful of sugar, a glass of sherry, a dessert-spoonful of lemon juice, and a small bunch of parsley. To one large flounder put a quart of water, and if you are going to jelly oysters put in their liquor and a little salt. Stew long and slowly, skimming well; then strain, and if not perfectly clear clarify as elsewhere directed. (See if your stock jellies, by trying it on ice before you clarify.) Now take a mold, put in it pieces of cold salmon, eels that have been cooked, or oysters, the latter only just cooked enough in the stock to plump them; pour a little of the jelly in the mold, then three or four half slices of lemon, then oysters or the cold fish, until the mold is near full, disposing the lemon so that it will be near the sides and decorate the jelly; then pour the rest of the jelly over all and stand in boiling water for a few minutes, then put it in a cold place, on ice is best, for some hours. When about to serve, dip the mold in hot water, turn out on a dish, garnish with lettuce leaves or parsley and hard-boiled eggs. The latter may be introduced into the jelly cut in quarters if it is desired; very ornamental force-meat balls made bright green with spinach juice are also an improvement in appearance.

A NEW MAYONNAISE (Soyer's).—Put a quarter of a pint of stiff veal jelly (that has been nicely flavored with vegetables) on ice in a bowl, whisking it till it is a white froth; then add half a pint of salad oil and six spoonfuls of tarragon vinegar, *by degrees*, first oil, then vinegar, continually whisking till it forms a white, smooth, sauce-like cream; season with half a teaspoonful of salt, a quarter ditto of white pepper, and a very little sugar, whisk it a little more and it is ready. It should be dressed pyramidically over the article it is served with. The advantage of this sauce is that (although more delicate than any other) you may dress it to any height you like, and it will remain so any length of time; if the temperature is cool, it will remain hours without appearing greasy or melting. It is absolutely necessary, however, that it should be prepared on ice.

All these dishes, however, are only adapted for large families, but there are several ways of improving on the ordinary lunch table of very small ones. And nothing is more pleasant for the mistress of one of these very small families than to have a friend drop in to lunch, and have a *recherché* lunch to offer with little trouble. Warming over will aid her in this, and to that chapter I refer her; but there are one or two ways of having cold relishes always ready, which help out an impromptu meal wonderfully.

Potted meats are a great resource to English housekeepers; this side the Atlantic they are chiefly known through the medium of Cross & Blackwell, though latterly one or two American firms have introduced some very admirable articles of the sort. Home-made potted meats are, however, better and less expensive than those bought; they should be packed away in jars, Liebig's extract of meat jars not being too small for the purpose, as, while covered with the fat they keep well; once opened, they require eating within a week or ten days, except in very cold weather.

Potted bloater is one of the least expensive and appetizing of all potted meats. To make it, take two or three or more bloaters, cut off the heads and cleanse them, put them in the oven long enough to cook them through; take them out, take off the skin, and remove the meat from the bones carefully; put the meat of the fish in a jar with half its weight of butter, leave it to *slowly* cook in a cool oven for an hour, then take it out, put the fish into a mortar or strong dish, pour the butter on it carefully, but don't let the gravy pass too, unless the fish is to be eaten very quickly, as it would prevent it keeping. Beat both butter and fish till they form a paste, add a little cayenne, and press it into small pots, pouring on each melted butter, or mutton suet. Either should be the third of an inch thick on the bloater. This makes excellent sandwiches.

POTTED HAM.—Take any remains of ham you have, even fried, if of a nice quality, is good for the purpose; take away all stringy parts, sinew, or gristle, put it in a slow oven with its weight of butter, let it stay macerating in the butter till very tender, then beat it in a mortar, add cayenne, and pack in pots in the same way as the bloater. Thus you may pot odds and ends of any meat or fish you have, and as a little potted meat goes a long way, when you have a little lobster, a bit of chicken breast, or even cold veal, I advise you to use it in this way; you will then have a little stock of dainties in the house to fall back on at any time for unexpected calls—a very important thing in the country.

Potted chicken or veal requires either a little tongue or lean ham to give flavor; but failing these, a little ravigotte butter, beaten in after the meat is well pounded, is by no means a bad substitute.

Many people like the flavor of anchovies, but do not like the idea of eating raw fish; for these anchovy butter is very acceptable.

Take the anchovies out of the liquor in which they are packed, but do not wash them, put them in twice their weight of butter in a jar, which stand in boiling water; set all back of the stove for an hour, then pound, add cayenne, and pack in glasses.

Unexpected company to luncheon with a lady who has to eat that meal alone generally, and (as is the unwise way of such ladies) makes it a very slender meal, is one of the ordeals of a young housekeeper; company to lunch and nothing in the house. But there is generally a dainty luncheon in every house if you know how to prepare it; there certainly always will be if you keep your store-room supplied with the things I have named. Let the table be prettily laid at all times, then if you have potted meat and preserves, have them put on the table. Are there cold potatoes? If so cut them up into potato salad, if they are whole; if broken, warm them in a wine-glass of milk, a teaspoonful of flour, and a piece as large as an egg of *maître d'hôtel* butter. Have you such scraps of cold meat as could not come to table? Toss them up with a half cup of water, a slice of glaze (oh, blessed ever-ready glaze!) a teaspoonful of ravigotte, or *maître d'hôtel*, and a teaspoonful of roux or blanc, according as your meat is light or dark, season, and serve. Or you have no meat, then you have eggs, and what better than an omelet and such an omelet as the following? Take the crumb of a slice of bread, soak it in hot milk (cold will do, but hot is better), beat up whites of four eggs to a high froth; mix the bread with all the milk it will absorb, *no more,* into a paste, add the yolks of eggs with a little salt, set the pan on the fire with an ounce of butter. Let it get very hot, then mix the whites of eggs with the yolks and bread lightly, pour in the pan, and move about for a minute; if the oven is hot, when the omelet is brown underneath, set the pan in the oven for five minutes, or until the top is set; then double half over, and serve. If your guests have a liking for sweets, and your potted meats supply the savory part of your luncheon, then have a brown gravy ready to serve with it. Put into a half cup of boiling water a slice of glaze, a spoonful of roux, and enough Harvey sauce, or mushroom powder, to flavor. If your omelet is to be sweet, before you fold it put in a layer of preserves.

The advantage of the omelet I have here given is that it keeps plump and tender till cold, so that five minutes of waiting does not turn it into leather, the great objection with omelets generally.

Potatoes for luncheon, as I have said, should always be prepared in some fancy way, and snow is a very pretty one. Have some fine mealy potatoes boiled, carefully poured off, and set back of the stove with a cloth over them till they are quite dry and fall apart; then have a colander, or coarse wire sieve made *hot* and a *hot* dish in which to serve them, pass the floury potatoes through the sieve, taking care not to crush the snow as it falls. You require a large dish heaping full. and be careful it is kept hot.

This mode of preparing potatoes, although very pretty and novel, must never be attempted with any but the whitest and mealiest kind.

The remains of cold potatoes may be prepared thus: Put three ounces of butter in a frying-pan in which fry three onions sliced till tender, but not very brown, then put on the potatoes cut in slices, and shake them till they are of a nice brown color, put a spoonful of chopped parsley, salt, pepper, and juice of a lemon, shake well that all may mix together, dish, and serve very hot.

CHAPTER VI.

A CHAPTER ON GENERAL MANAGEMENT IN VERY SMALL FAMILIES.

A VERY small family, "a young *ménage*," for instance, is very much more difficult to cater for without waste than a larger one; two people are so apt to get tired of anything, be it ever so good eating, when it has been on the table once or twice; therefore it would be useless to make galantine or the large pies I have indicated, except for occasions when guests are expected; but, as I hope to aid young housekeepers to have nice dishes when alone, I will devote this chapter to their needs.

The chapter on "Warming Over" will be very useful also to this large class.

In the first place it is well to have regard, when part of a dish leaves the table, as to whether it, or any particular part of it, will make a nice little cold dish, or a *rechauffé*; in that case have it saved, unless it is required for the servants' dinner (it is well to manage so that it is not needed for that purpose); for instance, if there is the wing and a slice or two of the breast of a chicken left, it will make a dainty little breakfast dish, or cold, in jelly, be nice for lunch. There is always jelly if you have roast chicken, if you manage properly, and this is how you do it:

Carefully save the feet, throat, gizzard, and liver of your chickens; scald the feet by pouring boiling water over them; leave them just a minute, and pull off the outer skin and nails; they come away very readily, leaving the feet delicately white; put these with the other giblets, properly cleansed, into a small saucepan with an onion, a slice of carrot, a sprig of parsley, and a pint of water (if you have the giblets of one chicken), if of two, put a quart; let this *slowly* simmer for two hours and a half; it will be reduced to about half, and form a stiff jelly when cold; a glass of sherry, and squeeze of lemon, or teaspoonful of tarragon vinegar, makes this into a delicious aspic, and should be added if to be eaten cold. The jelly must of course be strained.

In roasting chickens, if you follow the rule for meat, that is, put no water in the pan, but a piece of butter, and dredge a *very little* flour over the chicken, you will have a nice brown glaze at the bottom of the pan, provided it has been cooked in a *quick oven;* if in a cool oven there will be nothing brown at all; but we will suppose the bird is browned to a turn; pour your gravy from the giblets into the pan, take off every bit of the glaze or osmazone that adheres, and let it dissolve, rubbing it with the back of the spoon; then, if you are likely to have any chicken left cold, pour off a little gravy in a cup through a fine strainer, leaving in your pan sufficient for the dinner; in this mash up the liver till it is a smooth paste which thickens the gravy, and serve. Some object to liver, therefore the use of it is a matter of taste. If you dress the chickens English fashion, you will *need* the liver and gizzard to tuck under the wings; in this case, stew only the feet and throat, using a little meat of any kind, if you have it, to take their place; but on no account fail to use the feet, as they are as rich in jelly as calves' feet in proportion to their size.

General Management in Small Families. 49

The jelly laid aside will be enough to ornament and give relish to a little dish of cold chicken, and changes it from a dry and commonplace thing to a *recherché* one. If two chickens are cooked it is more economical than one; there is, then, double the amount of gravy, generally sufficient, if you lay some very nice pieces of cold chicken in a bowl, to pour over it and leave it enveloped in jelly; you still then, if from dinner for two people, have perhaps joints enough to make a dish of curry or fricassee, or any of the many ways in which cold chicken may be used, for which see chapter on *"Warming Over."*

For small households large joints are to be avoided, but even a small roast is a large joint when there are but two or three to eat it. For this reason it is a good plan to buy such joints as divide well. A sirloin of beef is better made into two fine dishes than into one roast, and then warmed over twice. Every one knows that *"Filet de bœuf Chateaubriand"* is one of the classical dishes of the French table, that to a Frenchman luxury can go no further; but every one does not know how entirely within his power it is to have that dish as often as he has roast beef; how convenient it would be to so have it. Here it is: When your sirloin roast comes from the butcher, take out the tenderloin or fillets, which you must always choose thick; cut it across into steaks an inch thick, trim them, cover them with a coat of butter (or oil, which is much better), and broil them ten minutes, turning them often; garnish with fried potatoes, and serve with *sauce Chateaubriand*, as follows: Put a gill of white wine (or claret will do if you have no white) into a saucepan, with a piece of glaze, weighing an ounce and a half; add three quarters of a pint of *espagnole*, and simmer fifteen minutes; when ready to serve, thicken with two ounces of *maître d'hôtel* butter in which a dessert-spoonful of flour has been worked. That is how Jules Gouffé's recipe runs; but, as no small family will keep *espagnole* ready made, allow a little more glaze (of course the recipe as given may be divided to half or quarter, provided the correct proportions are retained), and use a tablespoonful of roux and the *maître d'hôtel* butter, both of which you have probably in your store-room; if not, brown a little flour, chop some parsley, and add to two ounces of butter; work them together, then let them dissolve in the sauce, for which purpose let it go off the boil; let the sauce simmer a minute, skim, and serve.

The sirloin of beef, denuded of its fillet, is still a good roast; and as you can't have your cake and eat it too, and hot fresh roast beef is better than the same warmed over, warm ye never so wisely, I think this plan may commend itself to those who like nice *little* dinners.

A nice little dinner of a soup, an *entrée*, or made dish, salad, and dessert, really costs no more than frequent roast meat, or even steak and pudding, by following some such plan as this:

Sunday.—*Pot-au-feu* and roast lamb, leg of mutton or other good joint, etc.

Monday.—Rice or vermicelli soup made with remains of the *bouillon* from *pot-au-feu*. If the Sunday joint was a fore or hindquarter of lamb it should have been divided, say the leg from the loin, thus providing choice roasts for two days, and yet having enough cold lamb— that favorite dish with so many—for luncheon with a salad; and, surprising to say, after hot roast lamb for dinner Sunday, cold lunch for Monday, another roast Monday, and cold or warmed up for lunch Tuesday, there will still be (supposing as I do, in preparing this chapter, that the family consists only of gentleman, lady, and servant) remains enough from the two cold joints to make cromesquis of lamb (see recipe), a little dish of mince, or a delicate *sauté* of lamb for breakfast. It is surprising what may be done with odds and ends in a small family; a tiny plate of pieces, far too small to make an appearance on the table, and which, if special directions are not given, will seem to Bridget not worth saving, will, with each piece dipped into the batter *à la Carême*, and fried in hot fat, make a tempting dish for breakfast, or an *entrée* for dinner or luncheon. Two tablespoonfuls only of chopped meat of any kind will make croquettes for two or three people; hence, 'save the pieces.' But to return to our bills of fare: I have given the two roasts of lamb for consecutive days, because the weather in lamb season is usually too warm to keep it; when this can be done, however, it is pleasanter to leave the second joint of lamb till Tuesday. Should a forequarter (abroad held in greater esteem than the hindquarter) have been chosen, get the butcher to take out the shoulder in one round thick joint, English fashion; this crisply roasted is far more delicious than the leg; you then have the chops to be breaded, and an excellent dish of the neck and breast, either broiled, curried, stewed with peas, or roast.

Yet how often we see a whole quarter of lamb put in the oven for two or three people who get tired of the sight of it cold, yet feel in economy bound to eat it.

Should sirloin of beef have been the Sunday dinner, you will know what to do with it, from directions already given; and as a sirloin of beef, even with the fillet out, will be more than required for one dinner, it may serve for a third day, dressed in one of the various ways I shall give in chapter on "Warming Over." You have still at your disposal the bouilli or beef from which you have made your *pot-au-feu*, which, if it has been carefully boiled, not galloped, nor allowed to fall to rags, is very good eating. Cut thin with lettuce, or in winter celery, in about equal quantities, and a good salad dressing, it is excellent; or, made into hash, fritadella, or even rissoles, is savory and delicious; only bear in mind with this, as all cooked meats, the gravy drawn out must be replaced by stock or glaze; it is very easy to warm over bouilli satisfactorily, as a cup of the soup made from it can always be kept for gravy.

A leg of mutton makes two excellent joints, and is seldom liked cold—as beef and lamb often are.

Select a large fine leg, have it cut across, that each part may weigh about equally; roast the thick or fillet end and serve with or without onion sauce (*à la soubise*); boil the knuckle in a small quantity of water, just enough to cover it, with a carrot, turnip, onion, and bunch of parsley, and salt in the water, serve with caper sauce and mashed turnips. The broth from this is excellent soup served thus: Skim it carefully, take out the vegetables, and chop a small quantity of parsley very fine, then beat up in a bowl two eggs, pour into them a little of the broth—not boiling—beating all the time, then draw your soup back till it is off the boil, and pour in the eggs, stirring continually till it is on the boiling point again (but it must not boil, or the eggs will curdle and spoil the soup), and then turn it into a *hot* tureen and serve. Use remains of the cold roast and boiled mutton together, to make made dishes; between the days of having the roast and boiled mutton you may have had a fowl, and the remains from that will make you a second dish to go with your joint.

The remains from the first cooked mutton, in form of curry, mince, salmi, or *sauté*, will be a second dish with your fowl.

Veal is one of the most convenient things to have for a small family, as it warms over in a variety of ways, and in some is actually better than when put on the table as a joint. By having a little fish one day, instead of soup, and a little game another, and remembering when you have an especially dainty thing, to have one with it a little more substantial and less costly, you may have variety at little expense.

For instance, if you find it convenient to have for dinner fritadelle (see "*Warming Over*") or miroton of beef, or cold mutton curried, you might have broiled birds, or roast pigeon, or game. In this consists good management, to live so that the expenses of one day balance those of the other—unless you are so happily situated that expense is a small matter, in which case these remarks will not apply to you at all. Then, never mind warming over, or making one joint into two; let your poor neighbors and Bridget's friends enjoy your superfluity. To the woman with a moderate income it usually is a matter of importance, or ought to be, that her weekly expenditure should not exceed a certain amount, and for this she must arrange that any extra expense is balanced by a subsequent economy.

Salads add much to the health and elegance of a dinner; it is in early spring an expensive item if lettuce is used; but no salad can be more delicious or more healthful than dressed celery; and by buying when cheap, arranging with a man to lay in your cellar, covered with soil, enough for the winter's use, it need cost but moderately. Celeraic, or turnip-rooted celery is another salad that is very popular with our German friends; it is a bulbous celery, the root being the part eaten; these are cooked like potatoes, cut in slices, and dressed with oil and vinegar, or mayonnaise, it is exceedingly good. Potato salad is always procurable, and in summer at lunch, instead of the hot vegetable, or in winter when green salad is dear, is very valuable. It may be varied by the addition, one day, of a few chopped pickles, another, a little onion, or celery, or parsley, or tarragon, a little ravigotte butter beaten to cream with the vinegar, or with meat, as follows : Boil the potatoes in their skins, peel them, cut them into pieces twice the thickness of a fifty-cent piece, and put them into a salad bowl with cold meat (bouilli from soup is excellent); put to them a teaspoonful of salt, half that quantity of pepper, two tablespoonfuls of vinegar, three or even four of oil, and a teaspoonful of chopped parsley. You can vary this by putting at different times some chopped celery or pickles, olives, or anchovies.

CHAPTER VII.

ON FRYING AND BROILING.

FRYING is one of the operations in cookery in which there are more failures than any other, or, at least, there appear to be more, because the failure is always so very apparent. Nothing can make a dish of breaded cutlets on which are bald white spots look inviting, or livid-looking fish, just flaked here and there with the bread that has been persuaded to stay on. And, provided you have enough fat in the pan—there should always be enough to immerse the article; therefore use a deep iron or enameled pan—there can be but two reasons why you fail. Your fat has not been hot enough, or your crumbs have not been fine and *even*.

Many suppose when the fat bubbles and boils in the pan that it is quite hot; it is far from being so. Others again are so much nearer the truth that they know it must become *silent*, that is, boil and cease to boil, before it is ready, but even that is not enough; it must be silent some time, smoke, and appear to be on the point of burning, then drop a bit of bread in; if it crisps and takes color directly, quickly put in your articles.

These articles, whether cutlets or fish, must have been carefully prepared, or herein may lie the second cause of failure. Any cookery book will give you directions how to crumb, follow them; but what some do not tell you is, that your bread-crumbs should be *finely sifted;* every coarse crumb is liable to drop off and bring with it a good deal of the surrounding surface.

I also follow the French plan in using the egg, and mix with it oil and water in the proportion of three eggs, one tablespoonful of oil, one of water, and a little salt, beat together and use. It is a good plan to keep a supply of *panure* or dried bread-crumbs always ready. Cut any slices of baker's bread, dry them in a cool oven so that they remain quite colorless, or they will not do for the purpose. When as dry as crackers, crush under a rolling-pin, and sift; keep in a jar for use.

In no branch of cooking is excellence more appreciated than in that of frying. A dish of *filets de sole* or cutlets, crisp and golden brown, is an ornament to any table, and is seldom disdained by any one. Apropos of *filets de sole;* it is very high-sounding yet very attainable, as I shall show. I was staying with a friend early in spring, a lady always anxious for table novelties. "Oh, do tell me what fish to order, I should like something fried, now that you are here to tell cook how to do it; she hasn't the wildest idea, although she would be astounded to hear me say so." "Have you ever had flounders?" I asked. "Flounders!" My friend's pretty nose went up the eighth of an inch, and her confidence in my powers as counselor went down to zero. "Flounders! but they are a very common fish you know." "I know they are very delicious," I answered. "Order them, and trust me; but I must coax the autocrat of your kitchen to allow me to cook and prepare them myself."

An hour before dinner I went into the kitchen, put at least a pound of lard into a deep frying-pan, and set it where it would get gradually hot, then I turned my attention to the fish; they were thick, firm flounders, and were ready cleaned, scraped, and the heads off. I then proceeded to bone one in the following way : Take a sharp knife and split the flounder right down the middle of the back, then run the knife carefully between the flesh and bones going toward the edge. You have now detached one quarter of the flesh from the bone, do the other half in the same way, and when the back is thus entirely loose from the bone, turn the fish over and do the same with the other part. You will now find you can remove the bone whole from the fish, detaching, as you do so, any flesh still retaining the bone, then you have two halves of the fish; cut away the fins, and you have four quarters of solid fish. Now see if the fat is very hot, set it forward while you wipe your fish dry, and dip each piece in milk, then in flour. Try if the fat is hot by dropping a crumb into it; if it browns at once, put in the fish. When they are beautifully brown, which will be in about ten minutes, take them up in the colander, and then lay them on a towel to absorb any fat, lay them on a hot dish, and garnish with slices of lemon and parsley or celery tops.

Now when this dish made its appearance, my friend's husband, a *bon vivant*, greeted it with, "Aha! *Filets de sole à la Delmonico*," and as nothing to the contrary was said until dinner was over, he ate them under the impression that they were veritable *filets de sole*. Of course I can't pretend to say whether M. Delmonico imports his soles, or uses the homely flounder; but I do know that one of his frequenters knew no difference.

Oysters should be laid on a cloth to drain thoroughly, then rolled in fine sifted cracker dust, and dropped into very hot fat; do not put more oysters in the pan than will fry without one overlapping the other. Very few minutes will brown them beautifully, if your fat was hot enough, and as a minute too long toughens and shrinks them, be very careful that it browns a cube of bread almost directly, before you begin the oysters. Egg and bread-crumb may be used instead of cracker dust, but it is not the proper thing, and is a great deal more trouble. Should you be desirous of using it, however, the oysters must be carefully wiped *dry* before dipping them; while for cracker dust they are not wiped, but only drained well.

Fish of any kind, fried in batter *à la Carême* (see recipe), is very easy to do, and very nice.

Carefully save veal, lamb, beef, and pork drippings. Keep a crock to put it in, and, clarified as I shall direct, it is much better than lard for many purposes, and for frying especially; it does not leave the dark look that is sometimes seen on articles fried in lard. The perfection of "friture," or frying-fat, according to Gouffé, is equal parts of lard and beef fat melted together.

Yet there are families where dripping is never used—is looked upon as unfit to use—while the truth is that many persons quite unable to eat articles fried in lard would find no inconvenience from those fried in beef fat. It is as wholesome as butter, and far better for the purpose. Butter, indeed, is only good for frying such things as omelets or scrambled eggs; things that are cooked in a very short time, and require no great degree of heat.

The same may be said of oil, than which, for fish, nothing can be better. Yet it can only be used once, and is unsuitable for things requiring long-sustained heat, as it soon gets bitter and rank.

Do not be afraid to put a pound or two of fat in your pan for frying; it is quite as economical as to put less for it can be used over and over again, a pail or crock being kept for the purpose of receiving it. Always in returning it to the crock pour it through a fine strainer, so that no sediment or brown particles may pass which would spoil the next frying.

To clarify dripping, when poured from the meat-pan, it should go into a bowl, instead of the crock in which you wish to keep it. Then pour into the bowl also some boiling water, and add a little salt, stir it, and set it away. Next day, or when cold, run a knife round the bowl, and (unless it is pork) it will turn out in a solid cake, leaving the water and impurities at the bottom. Now scrape the bottom of your dripping, and put it in more boiling water till it melts, then stir again, another pinch of salt add, and let it cool again. When you take off the cake of fat, scrape it as before, and it is ready to be melted into the general crock, and will now keep for months in cool weather. If you are having frequent joints it is as well to do all your dripping together, once a week; but do not leave it long at any season with water under it, as that would taint it. Fat skimmed from boiled meat, *pot-au-feu*, before the vegetables, etc., go in, is quite as good as that from roast, treated in the same way.

Frying in batter is very easy and excellent for some things, such as warming over meat, being far better than eggs and crumbs. Carême gives the following recipe, which is excellent:

Three quarters of a pound of sifted flour, mixed with two ounces of butter melted in warm water; blow the butter off the water into the flour first, then enough of the water to make a *soft* paste, which beat smooth, then more warm water till it is batter thick enough to mask the back of a spoon dipped into it, and salt to taste; add the *last thing* the whites of two eggs well beaten.

Another batter, called *à la Provençale*, is also exceedingly good, especially for articles a little dry in themselves, such as chickens to be warmed over, slices of cold veal, etc.

Take same quantity of flour, two yolks of eggs, four tablespoonfuls of oil, mix with *cold* water, and add whites of eggs and salt as before. Into this batter I sometimes put a little chopped parsley, and the least bit of powdered thyme, or grated lemon-peel, or nutmeg; this is, however, only a matter of taste.

BROILING is the simplest of all forms of cooking, and is essentially English. To broil well is very easy with a little attention. A brisk clear fire, not too high in the stove, is necessary to do it with ease; yet if, as must sometimes happen, to meet the necessities of other cooking, your fire is very large, carefully fix the gridiron on two bricks or in any convenient manner, to prevent the meat scorching, then have the gridiron *very hot* before putting your meat upon it; turn it, if chop or steak, as soon as the gravy begins to start on the upper side; if allowed to remain without turning long, the gravy forms a pool on the top, which, when turned, falls into the fire and is lost; the action of the heat, if turned quickly, seals the pores and the gravy remains in the meat. If the fire is not very clear, put a cover over the meat on the gridiron, it will prevent its blackening or burning—if the article is thick I always do so—and it is an especially good plan with birds or chickens, which are apt to be raw at the joints unless this is done; indeed, with the latter, I think it a good way to put them in a hot oven ten minutes before they go on to broil, then have a spoonful of *maître d'hôtel* butter to lay on the breast of each. Young spring chickens are sometimes very dry, in which case dip them in melted butter, or, better still, oil them all over a little while before cooking. There is nothing more unsightly than a sprawling dish of broiled chickens; therefore, in preparing them place them in good form, then, with a gentle blow of the rolling-pin, break the bones that they may remain so.

CHAPTER VIII.

ROASTING.

In spite of Brillat-Savarin's maxim that one may become a cook, but must be born a *rotisseur*, I am inclined to think one may also, by remembering one or two things, become a very good "roaster" (to translate the untranslatable), especially in our day, when the oven has taken the place of the spit, although a great deal of meat is spoiled in roasting; a loin of lamb or piece of beef, that comes to the table so pale that you can't tell whether it has been boiled or merely wilted in the oven, is an aggravation so familiar, that a rich brown, well-roasted joint is generally a surprise. Perhaps the cook will tell you she has had the "hottest kind of an oven;" but then she has probably also had a well of water underneath it, the vapor from which, arising all the time, has effectually soddened the meat, and checked the browning. The surface of roast meat should be covered with a rich glaze, scientifically called "osmazone." That the meat may be thus glazed, it should always go into a *hot* oven, so that, as the gravy exudes, it may congeal on the outside, thus sealing up the pores. The general plan, however, is to put meat into a warm oven an hour or two earlier than it should go, with a quantity of water and flour underneath it. The result in hot weather I have known to be very disagreeable, the tepid oven having, in fact, given a stale taste to the joint before it began to cook, and it at all times results in flavorless, tough meat. There is no time saved, either, in putting the meat in while the oven is yet cool. Heat up the oven till it is quite brisk, then put the meat in a pan, in which, if it is fat, you require *no water;* if very lean, you may put half a teacup, just enough to prevent the pan burning; you may rub a little flour over the joint or not, as you please, but never more than the surface moisture absorbs; have no clinging particles of flour upon the joint, neither put salt nor pepper upon the meat before it goes into the oven; salt draws out the gravy, which it is your object to keep in, and the flavor of pepper is entirely changed by the parching it undergoes when on the surface of the meat, the odor of scorched pepper, while cooking, being very offensive to refined nostrils. This does not occur when pepper is not on the surface; for the *inside* of birds, in stuffing, and in meat pies it is indispensable, and the flavor undergoes no change. This remark on pepper applies also to broiling and frying. Always pepper *after* the article is cooked, and both for appearance and delicacy of flavor white pepper should always be used in preference to black.

Meat, while in the oven, should be carefully turned about so that it may brown equally, and when it has been in half the time you intend to give it, or when the upper surface is well browned, turn it over. When it comes out of the oven put it on a hot dish, then carefully pour off the fat by holding the corner of the meat pan over your dripping-pan, and very gently allowing the fat to run off; do not shake it; when you see the thick brown sediment beginning to run too, check it; if there is still much fat on the surface, take it off with a spoon; then pour into the pan a little boiling water and salt, in quantity according to the quantity of sediment or glaze in the pan, and with a spoon rub off every speck of the dried gravy on the bottom and sides of the pan. Add no flour, the gravy must be thick enough with its own richness. If you have added too much water, so that it looks poor, you may always boil it down by setting the pan on the stove for a few minutes; but it is better to put very little water at first, and add as the richness of the gravy allows. Now you have a rich brown gravy, instead of the thick whitey-brown broth so often served with roast meat. Every drop of this gravy and that from the dish should be carefully saved if left over.

Save all dripping, except from mutton or meat with which onions are cooked, for purposes which I shall indicate in another place.

Veal and pork require to be very thoroughly cooked. For them, therefore, the oven must not be too hot, neither must it be lukewarm, a good even heat is best; if likely to get too brown before it is thoroughly cooked, open the oven door.

CHAPTER IX.

BOILING.

Boiling is one of the things about which cooks are most careless; theoretically they almost always know meat should be slowly boiled, but their idea of "slow" is ruled by the fire; they never attempt to rule that. There is a good rule given by Gouffé as to what slow boiling actually is: the surface of the pot should only show signs of ebullition at one side, just an occasional bubble. *Simmering* is a still slower process, and in this the pot should have only a sizzling round one part of the edge. All fresh meat should boil *slowly;* ham or corn beef should barely simmer. Yet they must not go off the boil at all, which would spoil fresh meat entirely; steeping in water gives a flat, insipid taste.

All vegetables except potatoes, asparagus, peas, and cauliflower should boil as fast as possible; these four only moderately. Most vegetables are boiled far too long. Cabbage is as delicate as cauliflower in the summer and fall if boiled in plenty of water, to which a salt spoonful of soda has been added, as *fast as possible* for twenty minutes or half an hour, then drained and dressed. In winter it should be cut in six or eight pieces, boiled *fast*, in plenty of water, for half an hour, *no longer*. Always give it plenty of room, let the water boil rapidly when you put it in the pot, which set on the hottest part of the fire to come to that point again, and you will have no more strong, rank, yellow stuff on your table, no bad odor in your house. Peas require no more than twenty minutes' boiling if young; asparagus the same; the latter should always be boiled in a saucepan deep enough to let it stand up in the water when tied up in bunches, for this saves the heads. Potatoes should be poured off the minute they are done, and allowed to stand at the back of the stove with a clean cloth folded over them. They are the only vegetable that should be put into *cold* water. When new, boiling water is proper. When quite ripe they are more floury if put in cold water.

Soups.—As I have before said, I do not pretend to give many recipes, only to tell you how to succeed with the recipes given in other books. I shall, therefore, only give one recipe which I know is a novelty and one for the foundation of all soups. In one sense I have done the latter already. The stock for glaze is an excellent soup before it is reduced; but I will also give Jules Gouffé's method of making *pot-au-feu*, it being a most beautifully clear soup.

It often happens, however, that you have sufficient stock from bones, trimmings of meat, and odds and ends of gravies, which may always be turned to account; but the stock from such a source, although excellent, will not always be clear; therefore, you must proceed with it in the following manner, unless you wish to use it for thick soup:

Make your stock boiling hot and skim well; then have ready the whites of three eggs (I am supposing you have three quarts of stock—one egg to a quart), to which add half a pint of cold water; whisk well together; then add half a pint of the boiling stock gradually, still whisking the eggs; then stir the boiling stock rapidly, pouring in the whites of eggs, etc.; as you do it, stir quickly till nearly boiling again, then take it from the fire, let it remain till the whites of eggs separate; then strain through a clean, fine cloth into a basin. This rule once learned will clear every kind of soup or jelly.

There are many people who are good cooks, yet fail in clear soup, which is with them semi-opaque, while it should be like sherry. The cause of this opacity is generally quick boiling while the meat is in. This gives it a milky appearance. After the stock is once made and clear, quick boiling will do no harm, but of course wastes the soup, unless resorted to for the purpose of making it stronger. A word here about coloring soup: Most persons resort to burnt sugar, and, very carefully used, it is not at all a bad makeshift. But how often have we a rich-looking soup put before us, the vermicelli appearing to repose under a lake of strong russet *bouillon*, but which, on tasting, we find suggestive of nothing but burnt sugar and salt, every bit of flavor destroyed by the acrid coloring. Sometimes stock made by the recipe for *pot-au-feu* (to follow) requires no color; this depends on the beef; but usually all soup is more appetizing in appearance for a little browning, and for this purpose I always use burnt onions in preference to anything else. If you have none in store when the soup is put on, put a small onion in the oven (or on the back of the stove; should you be baking anything the odor would taint); turn it often till it gets quite black, but not *charred*. Then put it to the soup; it adds a fine flavor as well as color, and you need not fear overdoing it.

Soup that is to be reduced must be very lightly salted; for this reason salt is left out altogether for glaze, as the reduction causes the water only to evaporate, the salt remains.

GOUFFÉ'S POT-AU-FEU.—Four pounds of lean beef, six quarts of water, six ounces of carrot, six of turnip, six of onion, half an ounce of celery, one clove, salt.

Put the meat on in cold water, and just before it comes to the boil skim it, and throw in a wineglass of cold water, skim again, and, when it is "on the boil," again throw in another wineglass of cold water; do this two or three times. The object of adding the cold water is to keep it just off the boil until all the scum has risen, as the boiling point is when it comes to the surface, yet once having boiled, the scum is broken up, and the soup is never so clear.

The meat must simmer slowly, *not boil*, for three hours before the vegetables are added, then for a couple of hours more.

It is necessary to be very exact in the proportions of vegetables; but, of course, after having weighed them for soups once or twice, you will get to know about the size of a carrot, turnip, etc., that will weigh six ounces. The exact weight is given until the eye is accustomed to it.

This soup strained, and boiled down to one half, becomes *consommé*.

CELERY CREAM is a most delicious and little-known white soup, and all lovers of good things will thank me for introducing it.

Have some nice veal stock, or the water in which chickens have been boiled, reduced till it is rich enough, will do, or some very rich mutton broth, but either of the former are preferable; then put on a half cup of rice in a pint of rich milk, and grate into it the white part and root of two heads of celery. Let the rice milk cook very slowly at the back of the stove, adding more milk before it gets at all stiff; when tender enough to mash through a coarse sieve or fine colander add it to the stock, which must have been strained and be quite free from sediment, season with salt and a little *white* pepper or cayenne, boil all together gently a few minutes. It should look like rich cream, and be strongly flavored with celery. Of course the quantity of rice, milk, and celery must depend on the quantity of stock you have. I have given the proportion for one quart, which, with the milk, etc., added, would make about three pints of soup.

CHAPTER X.

SAUCES.

TALLEYRAND said England was a country with twenty-four religions and only one sauce. He might have said two sauces, and he would have been literally right as regards both England and America. Everything is served with brown sauce or white sauce. And how often the white sauce is like bookbinder's paste, the brown, a bitter, tasteless brown mess! Strictly speaking, perhaps, the French have but two sauces either, *espagnole,* or brown sauce, and white sauce, which they call the mother sauces; but what changes they ring on these mother sauces! The espagnole once made, with no two meats is it served alike in flavor, and in this matter of flavor the artist appears. In making brown sauce for any purpose, bethink yourself of anything there may be in your store-room with which to vary its flavor, taking care that it shall agree with the meat for which it is intended. The ordinary cook flies at once to Worcestershire or Harvey sauce, which are excellent at times, but "*toujours perdrix*" is not always welcome. A pinch of mushroom powder, or a few chopped oysters, are excellent with beef or veal; so will be a spoonful of Montpellier butter stirred in, or curry, not enough to yellow the sauce, but enough to give a dash of piquancy. A pickled walnut chopped, or a gherkin or two, go admirably with mutton or pork chops. In short, this is just where

Sauces. 71

imagination and brains will tell in cooking, and little essays of invention may be tried with profit. But beware of trying too much; make yourself perfect in one thing before venturing on another.

ESPAGNOLE, or brown sauce, is simply a rich stock well flavored with vegetables and herbs, and thickened with a piece of *roux* or with brown flour.

WHITE SAUCE is one of those things we rarely find perfectly made; bad, it is the *ne plus ultra* of badness; good, it is delicious. Those who have tried to have it good, and failed, I beg to try the following method of making it: Take an ounce and a half of butter and a scant tablespoonful of flour, mix both with a spoon into a paste; when smooth add half a pint of warm milk, a *small* teaspoonful of salt, and the sixth part of one of *white* pepper; set it on the fire till it boils, and is thick enough to mask the back of the spoon transparently; then add a squeeze of lemon juice, and another ounce and a half of fresh butter; stir this till quite blended. This sauce is the foundation for many others, and, for some purposes, the beaten yolk of an egg is introduced when just off the boil. Capers may be added to it, or chopped mushrooms, or chopped celery, or oysters, according to the use for which it is intended. The object of adding the second butter is because boiling takes away the flavor of butter; by stirring half of it in, without boiling, you retain it.

CHAPTER XI.

WARMING OVER.

HASH is a peculiarly American institution. In no other country is every remnant of cold meat turned into that one unvarying dish. What do I say? *remnants* of cold meat! rather *joints* of cold meat, a roast of beef of which the tenderloin had sufficed for the first day's dinner, the leg of mutton from which a few slices only have been taken, the fillet of veal, available for so many delicate dishes, all are ruthlessly turned into the all-pervading hash. The curious thing is that people are not fond of it. Men exclaim against it, and its name stinks in the nostrils of those unhappy ones whose home is the boarding-house.

Yet hash in itself is not a bad dish; when I say it is a peculiarly *American* institution, I mean, that when English people speak of hash, they mean something quite different—meat warmed in slices. Our hash, in its best form—that is, made with nice gravy, garnished with sippets of toast and pickles, surrounded with mashed potatoes or rice—is dignified abroad by the name of *mince*, and makes its appearance as an elegant little *entrée*. Nor would it be anathematized in the way it is with us, if it were only occasionally introduced. It is the familiarity that has led to contempt. "But what shall I do?" asks the young wife distressfully;

"John likes joints, and he and I and Bridget can't possibly eat a roast at a meal."

Very true; and it is to just such perplexed young housekeepers that I hope this chapter will be especially useful—that is to say, small families with moderate means and a taste for good things. In this, as in many other ways, large families are easier to cater for; they can consume the better part of a roast at a meal, and the remains it is no great harm to turn into hash, although even they might, with little trouble and expense, have agreeable variety introduced into their bill of fare.

In England and America there is great prejudice against warmed-over food, but on the continent one eats it half the time in some of the most delicious-made dishes without suspecting it. Herein lies the secret. With us and our transatlantic cousins the warming over is so artlessly done, that the *hard* fact too often stares at us from out the watery expanse in which it reposes.

One great reason of the failure to make warmed-over meat satisfactory is the lack of gravy. On the goodness of this (as well as its presence) depends the success of your *réchauffé*.

The glaze, for which I have given the recipe, renders you at all times independent in this respect, but at the same time it should not alone be depended on. Every drop of what remains in the dish from the roast should be saved, and great care be taken of all scraps, bones, and gristle, which should be carefully boiled down to save the necessity of flying to the glaze for every purpose. I will here give several recipes, which I think may be new to many readers.

SALMI OF COLD MEAT is exceedingly good. Melt butter in a saucepan, if for quite a small dish two ounces will be sufficient; when melted, stir in a little flour to thicken; let it brown, but not burn, or, if you are preparing the dish in haste, put in some brown flour; then add a glass of white or red wine and a cup of broth, or a cup of water and a slice of glaze, a sprig or two of thyme, parsley, a small onion, chopped, and one bay leaf, pepper, and salt. Simmer all thoroughly (all savory dishes to which wine is added should simmer long enough for the distinct "winey" flavor to disappear, only the strength and richness remaining). Strain this when simmered half an hour and lay in the cold meat. Squeeze in a little lemon juice and draw the stew-pan to the back of the stove, but where it will cook no longer, or the meat will harden. Serve on toast, and pour the sauce over. A glass of brandy added to this dish when the meat goes in is a great addition, if an extra fine salmi is desired. By not allowing the flour and butter to brown and using white wine, this is a very fine sauce in which to warm cold chicken, veal, or any *white* meat.

BŒUF À LA JARDINIÈRE.—Put in a fireproof dish if you have it, or a thick saucepan, a pint of beef broth, a small bunch each of parsley, chervil, tarragon—very little of this—shallot or onion, capers, pickled gherkins, of each or any a teaspoonful chopped fine; roll a large tablespoonful of butter with a dessert-spoonful of brown flour, stir it in; then take slices of underdone beef, with a blunt knife hack each slice all over in fine dice, but not to separate or cut up the slices; then pepper and salt each one and lay it in with the herbs, sprinkle a layer of herbs over the beef and cover closely; then stand the dish in the oven to slowly cook for an hour, or, if you use a stew-pan, set in a pan of boiling water on the stove for an hour where the water will just boil. Serve on a dish surrounded with young carrots and turnips if in season, or old ones cut.

BEEF AU GRATIN.—Cut a little fat bacon or pork very thin, sprinkle on it chopped parsley, onion, and mushrooms (mushroom powder will do) and bread-crumbs; then put in layers of beef, cut thick, and well and closely hacked, then another layer of bacon or pork cut thin as a wafer, and of seasoning, crumbs last; pour over enough broth or gravy to moisten well, in which a little brandy or wine may be added if an especially good dish is desired; bake slowly an hour.

PSEUDO BEEFSTEAK.—Cut cold boiled or roast beef in thick slices, broil slowly, lay in a *hot* dish in which you have a large spoonful of Montpellier butter melted, sprinkle a little mushroom powder if you desire, and garnish with fried potato.

CUTLETS À LA JARDINIÈRE.—Trim some thick cutlets from a cold leg of mutton, or chops from the loin, dip them in frying batter, *à la Carême*, fry crisp and quickly, and serve wreathed round green peas, or a ragout made as follows: Take young carrots, turnips, green peas, white beans; stew gently in a little water to which the bones of the meat and trimmings have been added (and which must be carefully removed not to disfigure the vegetables). Encircle this ragout with the fried cutlets, and crown with a cauliflower.

CROMESQUIS OF LAMB is a Polish recipe. Cut some underdone lamb—mutton will of course do—quite small; also some mushrooms, cut small, or the powder. Put in a saucepan a piece of glaze the size of a pigeon's egg, with a *little* water or broth, warm it and thicken with yolks of two eggs, just as you would make boiled custard, that is, without letting it come to the boil, or it will curdle; then add the mushrooms and meat, let all get cold, and divide it into small pieces, roll in bread-crumbs sifted, then in egg, then in crumbs again, and fry in very hot fat; or you may, *after* rolling in bread-crumbs, lay each piece in a spoon and dip it into frying batter; let the extra batter run off, and drop the cromesquis into the hot fat. These will be good made of beef and rolled up in a bard of fat pork cut thin, and fried; serve with sauce piquant made thus: Take some chopped parsley, onion, and pickled cucumbers, simmer till tender, and thicken with an equal quantity of butter and flour. Of course your own brightness will tell you that, if you are in haste, a spoonful of Montpellier butter, the same of flour, melted in a little water, to which you add a teaspoonful of vinegar, will make an excellent sauce piquant, and this same is excellent for anything fried, as breaded chops, croquettes, etc. I may here say, that where two or three herbs are mentioned as necessary, for instance, parsley, tarragon, and chervil, if you have no tarragon you must leave it out, or chervil the same. It is only a matter of flavoring, at the same time *flavor* is a great deal, and these French herbs give that indescribable *cachet* to a dish which is one of the secrets of French cooking. Therefore if you are a wise matron you will have a supply on hand, even if only bought dry from the druggist.

MIROTON OF BEEF.—Peel and cut into thin slices two large onions, put them in a stew-pan with two ounces of butter, place it over a slow fire; stir the onions round till they are rather brown, but not in the least burnt; add a teaspoonful of brown flour, mix smoothly, then moisten with half a pint of broth, or water with a little piece of glaze, three salt-spoonfuls of salt unless your broth was salted, then half the quantity or less, two of sugar, and one of pepper. Put in the cold beef, cut in thin slices as lean as possible, let it remain five minutes at the back of the stove ; then serve on a very hot dish garnished with fried potatoes, or sippets of toast. To vary the flavor, sometimes put a spoonful of tarragon or plain vinegar, or a teaspoonful of mushroom powder, or a pinch of curry, unless objected to, or a few sweet herbs. In fact, as you may see, variety is as easy to produce as it is rare to meet with in average cooking, and depends more on intelligence and thoughtfulness than on anything else.

The simplest of all ways of warming a joint that is not far cut, is to wrap it in thickly buttered paper, and put it in the oven again, contriving, if possible, to cover it closely, let it remain long enough to get *hot* through, not to cook. By keeping it closely covered it will get hot through in less time, and the steam will prevent it getting hard and dry ; make some gravy hot and serve with the meat. If your gravy is good and plentiful, your meat will be as nice as the first day; without gravy it would be an unsatisfactory dish. If you cannot manage to cover the joint in the oven, you may put it in a pot over the fire *without* water, but with a dessert spoonful of vinegar to create steam ; let it get hot through, and serve as before.

For the third day the meat may be warmed up in any of the ways I am going to mention, repeating once more, that you must have gravy of some kind, or else carefully make some, with cracked bones, gristle, etc., stewed *long*, and nicely flavored with any kind of sauce.

RAGOUT.—A very nice ragout may be made from cold meat thus: Slice the meat, put it in a stew-pan in which an onion, or several if you like them, has been sliced; squeeze half a lemon into it, or a dessert-spoonful of vinegar, cover closely without water, and when it begins to cook, set the stew-pan at the back of the stove for three quarters of an hour, shaking it occasionally. The onions should now be brown; take out the meat, dredge in a little flour, stir it round, and add a cup of gravy, pepper, salt, and a small quantity of any sauce or flavoring you prefer; stew gently a minute or two, then put the meat back to get hot, and serve; garnish with sippets of toast, or pickles.

A NICE LITTLE BREAKFAST DISH is made thus: Cut two long slices of cold meat and three of bread, buttered thickly, about the same shape and size; season the meat with pepper, salt, and a little finely chopped parsley; or, if it is veal, a little chopped ham; then lay one slice of bread between two of meat, and have the other two slices outside; fasten together with short wooden skewers. If you have a quick oven, put it in; and take care to baste with butter thoroughly, that the bread may be all over crisp and brown. If you can't depend on your oven, fry it in very hot fat as you would crullers; garnish with sprigs of parsley, and serve very hot.

TO WARM A GOOD-SIZED PIECE OF BEEF.—Trim it as much like a thick fillet as you can; cut it horizontally half way through, then scoop out as much as you can of the meat from the inside of each piece. Chop the meat fine that you have thus scooped out, season with a little finely chopped parsley and thyme, a shred of onion, if you like it; or if you have celery boil a little of the coarser part till tender, chop it and add as much bread finely crumbled as you have meat, and a good piece of butter; add pepper and salt, and make all into a paste with an egg, mixed with an equal quantity of gravy or milk; fill up the hollow in the meat and tie, or still better, sew it together. You may either put this in a pot with a slice of pork or bacon, and a cup of gravy; or you may brush it over with beaten egg, cover it with crumbs, and pour over these a cup of butter, melted, so that it moistens every part; and bake it, taking care to baste well while baking; serve with nice gravy.

BEEF OLIVES are no novelty to the ear, but it is a novel thing to find them satisfactory to the palate.

Take some stale bread-crumbs, an equal quantity of beef finely chopped, some parsley, and thyme; a little scraped ham if you have it, a few chives, or a slice of onion, all chopped small as possible; put some butter in a pan, and let this force-meat just simmer, *not fry*, in it for ten minutes. While this is cooking, cut some underdone oblong slices of beef about half an inch thick, hack it with a sharp knife on *both sides;* then mix the cooked force-meat with the yolk of an egg and a tablespoonful of gravy; put a spoonful of this paste in the center of each slice of meat and tie it up carefully in the shape of an egg. Then if you have some nice gravy, thicken it with a piece of butter rolled in flour, roll each olive slightly in flour and lay it in the gravy and let it very gently *simmer* for half an hour. A few chopped oysters added to the gravy will be a great addition. Or you may lay each olive on a thin slice of fat pork, roll it up, tie it, dip it in flour, and bake in a quick oven until beautifully brown.

TO WARM OVER COLD MUTTON.—An excellent and simple way is to cut it, if loin, into chops, or leg, into thick collops, and dip each into egg well beaten with a tablespoonful of milk, then in *fine* bread-crumbs and fry in plenty of *very hot* fat.

If your crumbs are not very fine and even, the larger crumbs will fall off, and the appearance be spoilt. These chops will be almost as nice, if quickly fried, as fresh cooked ones. They will also be excellent if, instead of being breaded, they are dipped into thick batter (see recipe) and fried brown in the same way. This method answers for any kind of meat, chicken thus warmed over being especially good. The batter, or egg and bread-crumbs form a sort of crust which keeps it tender and juicy. Any attempt to fry cold meat without either results in a hard, stringy, uneatable dish.

WHITE MEAT OF ANY KIND is excellent warmed over in a little milk, in which you have cut a large onion, and, if you like it, a slice of salt pork or ham, and a little sliced cucumber, if it is summer; thicken with the yolks of one or two eggs, added after the whole has simmered twenty minutes; take care the egg thickens in the gravy, but does not *boil*, or it will curdle. If it is in winter, chop a teaspoonful of pickled cucumber or capers and add just on going to table. In summer when you have the sliced cucumber, squeeze half a lemon into the gravy, the last thing, to give the requisite dash of acid. You may vary the above by adding sometimes a few chopped oysters; at others, mushrooms, or celery. The last must be put in with the onion and before the meat.

DEVILED MEAT.—Our better halves are usually fond of this, especially for breakfast or lunch.

For this dish take a pair of turkey or chicken drumsticks or some nice thick wedges of underdone beef or mutton, score them deeply with a knife and rub them over with a sauce made thus: A teaspoonful of vinegar, the same of Harvey or Worcestershire sauce, the same of mustard, a *little* cayenne, and a tablespoonful of salad oil, or butter melted; mix all till like cream, and take care your meat is thoroughly moistened all over with the mixture, then rub your gridiron with butter. See that the fire is clear, and while the gridiron is getting hot, chop a teaspoonful of parsley very fine, mix it up with a piece of butter the size of a walnut, and lay this in a dish which you will put to get hot. Then put the meat to be grilled on the fire and turn often, so that it will not burn; when hot through and brown, lay it in the hot dish, lay another hot dish over it, and serve as quickly as possible with hot plates.

Or the grill may be served with what Soyer calls his *Mephistophelian sauce,* which he especially designed for serving with deviled meats. Chop six shallots or small onions, wash and press them in the corner of a clean cloth, put them in a stew-pan with half a wineglass of chili vinegar (pepper sauce), a chopped clove, a tiny bit of garlic, two bay leaves, an ounce of glaze; boil all together ten minutes; then add four tablespoonfuls of tomato sauce, a *little* sugar, and ten of broth thickened with roux (or water will do if you have no broth).

It will be remarked that in many French recipes a *little* sugar is ordered. This is not meant to sweeten, or even be perceptible; but it enriches, softens, tones, as it were, the other ingredients as salt does.

SOYER'S FRITADELLA (twenty recipes in one).—Put half a pound of bread-crumb to soak in a pint of cold water; take the same quantity of any kind of roast, or boiled meat, with a little fat, chop it fine, press the bread in a clean cloth to extract the water; put in a stew-pan two ounces of butter, a tablespoonful of chopped onions; fry two minutes and stir, then add the bread, stir and fry till rather dry, then the meat; season with a teaspoonful of salt, half of pepper, and a little grated nutmeg, and lemon peel; stir continually till very hot, then add two eggs, one at a time; mix well and pour on a dish to get cold. Then take a piece, shape it like a small egg, flatten it a little, egg and bread-crumb it all over, taking care to keep in good shape. Do all the same way, then put into a frying-pan a quarter of a pound of lard or dripping, let it get hot, and put in the pieces, and sauté (or as we call it "*fry*") them a fine yellow brown. Serve very hot with a border of mashed potatoes, or any garniture you fancy. Sauce piquant, or not, as you please.

The above can be made with any kind of meat, poultry, game, fish, or even vegetables; hard eggs, or potatoes, may be introduced in small quantities, and they may be fried instead of sautéed (frying in the French and strict sense, meaning as I need hardly say, entire immersion in very hot fat). To *fry* them you require at least two pounds of fat in your pan.

Oysters or lobsters prepared as above are excellent.

Boileau says, "*Un diner réchauffé ne valut jamais rien.*" But I think a good French cook of the present day would make him alter his opinion.

Indeed Savarin quotes a friend of his own, a notable gourmand, who considered spinach cooked on Monday only reached perfection the following Saturday, having each day of the week been warmed up with butter, and each day gaining succulence and a more marrowy consistency.

The only trouble I find in relation to this part of my present task is the difficulty of knowing when to leave off. There are so many ways of warming meats to advantage—and in every one way there is the suggestion for another—that I suffer from an *embarras de richesse*, and have had difficulty in selecting. Dozens come to my mind, blanquettes, patties, curries, as I write; but as this is not, I have said, to be a recipe book, I forbear. Of one thing I am quite sure : when women once know how to make nice dishes of cold meat they will live well where they now live badly, and for less money; and "hash" will be relegated to its proper place as an occasional and acceptable dish.

CHAPTER XII.

ON FRIANDISES.

"Le rôle du gourmand finit avec l'entremets, et celui du friand commence au dessert.—*Grimod de la Reyniere.*

AMERICAN ladies, as a rule, excel in cake making and preserving, and I feel that on that head I have very little to teach; indeed, were they as accomplished in all branches of cooking as in making dainty sweet dishes this book would be uncalled for.

Yet, notwithstanding their undoubted taste and ability in making "*friandises,*" it seems to me a few recipes borrowed from what the French call *la grande cuisine,* and possible of execution at home, will be welcome to those who wish to vary the eternal ice cream and charlotte russe, with other sweets more elegant and likely to be equally popular.

ICED SOUFFLÉ À LA BYRON.—One pint of sugar syrup of 32 degrees (get this at a druggist's if you do not understand sugar boiling), three gills of strained raspberry juice, one lemon, one gill of maraschino, fifteen yolks of eggs, two ounces of chocolate drops, half a pint of very thick cream whipped.

Method of making this and the next recipe is as follows: Mix the syrup and yolks of eggs, strain into a warm bowl, add the raspberry and lemon juice and maraschino, whisk till it creams well, then take the bowl out of the hot water and whisk ten minutes longer; add the chocolate drops and whipped cream; lightly fill a case or mold, and set in a freezer for two hours, then cover the surface with lady-fingers (or sponge cake) dried in the oven a pale brown, and rolled. Serve at once.

Another frozen *soufflé* is as follows:

One pint of syrup, 32 degrees, half a pint of noyeau, half a pint of cherry juice, two ounces of bruised macaroons, half a pint of thick cream whipped, made in the same way as the last. I may here say that the fruit juices can be procured now at all good druggists, so that these *soufflés* are very attainable in winter, and as noyeau and maraschino do not form part of the stores in a family of small means, I will give in this chapter recipes for the making of very fair imitations of the genuine *liqueurs*.

BISCUIT GLACÉ À LA CHARLES DICKENS.—One pint of syrup (32°), fifteen yolks of eggs, three gills of peach pulp, colored pink with cochineal, one gill of noyeau, half a pint of thick cream, and a little chocolate water-ice, made with half a pint of syrup and four ounces of the best chocolate smoothly mixed and frozen ready.

Mix syrup, yolks, peach pulps, noyeau, and a few drops of vanilla, whip high; mix with the whipped cream, and set in ice for one hour and a half in brick-shaped molds, then turn out (if very firm), and cut in slices an inch thick, and coat them all over, or on top and sides, with the chocolate ice, smoothing with a knife dipped in cold water; serve in paper cases.

BISCUIT GLACÉ À LA THACKERAY.—One pint of syrup (32°), one pint of strawberry pulp, fifteen yolks of eggs, one ounce of vanilla sugar (flavor a little sugar with vanilla), half a pint of thick cream.

Mix syrup, yolks, strawberry, and vanilla sugar, whipping as before, then add the whipped cream lightly; fill paper cases, either round or square; surround each with a band of stiff paper, to reach half an inch above the edge of the case, the bands to be pinned together to secure them; place them in a freezer. When about to send to table, remove the bands of paper, and cover with macaroons bruised fine and browned in the oven. The bands of paper are meant to give the biscuit the appearance of having risen while supposed to bake.

These delicious ices were invented by Francatelli, the Queen of England's chief cook, to do homage to the different great men whose names they bear, on the occasion of preparing dinners given in their honor. They read as if somewhat intricate, but any lady who has ever had ice cream made at home, and had the patience to make charlotte russe, need not shrink appalled before these novelties, or fear for a successful result.

Baba is a cake many call for at a confectioner's, yet few, if any one, attempts to make it at home. That the recipes generally offered do not lead to success may be one reason, and I offer the following, quite sure, if accurately followed, such a baba will result as never was eaten outside of Paris.

BABA.—One pound of flour; take one quarter of it, and make a sponge with half an ounce of compressed yeast and a little warm water, set it to rise, make a hole in the rest of the flour, add to it ten ounces of butter, three eggs, and a dessert-spoonful of sugar, a little salt, unless your butter salts it enough, which is generally the case. Beat all together well, then add five more eggs, one at a time, that is to say, add one egg and beat well, then another and beat again, and so on until the five are used. When the paste leaves the bowl it is beaten enough, but not before; then add the sponge to it, and a large half ounce of citron chopped, the same of currants, and an ounce and a half of sultana raisins, seedless. Let it rise to twice its size, then bake it in an oven of dark yellow paper heat; the small round babas are an innovation of the pastry-cook to enable him to sell them uncut. But the baba proper should be baked in a large, deep, upright tin, such as a large charlotte russe mold, when they keep for several days fresh, and if they get stale, make delicious fritters, soaked in sherry and dipped in frying batter.

In some cases, however, it may be preferred to make them as usually seen at French pastry cooks; for this purpose you require a dozen small-sized *round* charlotte russe molds, which fill half full only, as they rise very much; bake these in a hotter oven, light brown paper heat; try with a twig as you would any other cake, if it comes out dry it is done; then prepare a syrup as follows: Boil half pound of sugar in a pint of water, add to this the third of a pint of rum, and some apricot pulp—peach will of course do—and boil all together a few minutes; pour this half an inch deep in a dish, and stand the cake or cakes in it; it should drink up all the syrup, you may also sprinkle some over it. If any syrup remains, use it to warm over your cake when stale, instead of the sherry.

Baba was introduced into France by Stanislas Lecczinski, king of Poland, and the father-in-law of Louis XIV.; and his Polish royal descendants still use with it, says Carême, a syrup made of Malaga wine and one sixth part of *eau de tanaisie*.

But, although our forefathers seemed to have relished

tansy very much, to judge from old recipe books, I doubt if such flavoring would be appreciated in our time.

SAVARINS—commonly called wine cake by New York pastry cooks—are made as follows :

One pound of flour, of which take one quarter to make a sponge, using half an ounce of German compressed yeast, and a little warm milk ; when it has risen to twice its bulk, add one gill of hot milk, two eggs, and the rest of the flour ; mix well ; then add one more egg and beat, another, still beating; then add three quarters of a pound of fresh butter, a quarter of an ounce of salt, half an ounce of sugar, and half a gill of hot milk, beat well; then add eggs, one at a time, beating continually, until you have used five more. Cut in small dice three ounces of candied orange peel; butter a tin, which should be deep and straight-sided—a tin pudding boiler is not a bad thing—and sprinkle with chopped almonds. Fill the mold half full, and when risen to twice its bulk, bake in a moderate oven, dark yellow paper heat. When served, this cake should stand in a dish of syrup, flavored with rum, as for baba, or with sherry wine.

BOUCHÉES DES DAMES, a very ornamental and delicious little French cake, is sufficiently novel to deserve a place here, I think. Make any nice drop cake batter (either sponge, or sponge with a little butter in it I prefer) ; drop one on buttered paper and bake ; if it runs, beat in a *little* more flour and sugar, but not much, or your cakes will be brittle ; they should be the size, when done, of a fifty-cent piece, and I find half a teaspoonful of batter dropped generally makes them about right. Have a tin cutter or tin box lid, if you have no cutter so small, about the size, and with it trim each cake when baked ;

then take half the number and spread some with a very thin layer of red currant jelly, others with peach or raspberry; then on each so spread put a cake that is unspread, thus making a tiny sandwich or jelly cake. If you have different sorts of jelly, put each separate, as you must adapt the flavor of your icing to the jelly. For red currant, ice with chocolate icing. Recipes for icing are so general that I refer you to your cookery book. Those with peach may have white icing, flavored with almond, or with rum, beating in a little more sugar if the flavoring dilutes your icing too much. Almond flavoring goes well with raspberry. Cakes with raspberry jelly or jam should be iced pink, coloring the icing with prepared cochineal or cranberry juice. Thus you have your cakes brown, pink, and white, which look very pretty mixed.

The process of icing is difficult to do after they are put together, but they are much handsomer this way, and keep longer. You require, to accomplish it, a good quantity of each kind of icing, and a number of little wooden skewers; stick one into each cake and dip it in the icing, let it run off, then stand the other end of the skewer in a box of sand or granulated sugar. The easiest way is to ice each half cake before putting in the jelly; when the icing is hard spread with jelly, and put together.

CURAÇOA may be successfully imitated by pouring over eight ounces of the *thinly* pared rind of very ripe oranges a pint of boiling water, cover, and let it cool; then add two quarts of brandy, or strong French spirit, cover closely, and let it stand fourteen days, shaking it every day. Make a clarified syrup of two pounds of sugar into one pint of water, well boiled; strain the brandy into it, leaving it covered close another day. Rub up in a mortar one drachm of potash, with a teaspoonful of the liqueurs; when well blended, put this into the liqueur, and in the same way pound and add a drachm of alum, shake well, and in an hour or two filter through thin muslin. Ready for use in a week or two.

MARASCHINO.—Bruise slightly a dozen cherry kernels, put them in a deep jar with the outer rind of three oranges and two lemons, cover with two quarts of gin, then add syrup and leave it a fortnight, as for curaçoa. Stir syrup and spirit together, leave it another day, run it through a jelly bag, and bottle. Ready to use in ten days.

NOYEAU.—Blanch and pound two pounds of bitter almonds, or four of peach kernels; put to them a gallon of spirit or brandy, two pounds of white sugar candy—or sugar will do—a grated nutmeg, and a pod of vanilla; leave it three weeks covered close, then filter and bottle; but do not use it for three months. To be used with caution.

CHAPTER XIII.

FRENCH CANDY AT HOME.

This chapter I shall have to make one of recipes chiefly, for it treats of a branch of cooking not usually found in cookery books, or at least there is seldom anything on the art of confectionery beyond molasses or cream taffy and nougat. These, therefore, I shall not touch upon, but rather show you how to make the expensive French candies.

The great art of making these exquisite candies is in boiling the sugar, and it is an art easily acquired with patience.

Put into a marbleized saucepan (by long experience in sugar-boiling I find them less likely to burn even than brass, and I keep one for the purpose) one pound of sugar and half a pint of water; when it has boiled ten minutes begin to try it; have a bowl of water with a piece of ice near you, and drop it from the end of a spoon. When it falls to the bottom, and you can take it up and make it into a softish ball (not at all sticky) between your thumb and finger, it is at the right point; remove it from the fire to a cold place; when cool, if perfectly right, a thin jelly-like film will be over the surface, *not a sugary one;* if it is sugary, and you want your candy very creamy, you must add a few spoonfuls of water, return to the fire and boil again, going through the same process of trying it. You must be careful that there is not the least inclination to be brittle in the ball of candy you take from the water; if so, it is boiled a degree too high; put a little water to bring it back again, and try once more. A speck of cream of tartar is useful in checking a tendency in the syrup to go to sugar. When you have your sugar boiled just right set it to cool, and when you can bear your finger in it, begin to beat it with a spoon; in ten minutes it will be a white paste resembling lard, which you will find you can work like bread dough. This, then, is your foundation, called by French confectioners *fondant;* with your *fondant* you can work marvels. But to begin with the simplest French candies.

Take a piece of *fondant,* flavor part of it with vanilla, part of it with lemon, color yellow (see coloring candies), and another part with raspberry, color pink; make these into balls, grooved cones, or anything that strikes your fancy, let them stand till they harden, they are then ready for use.

Take another part of your *fondant,* have some English walnuts chopped, flavor with vanilla and color pink; work the walnuts into the paste as you would fruit into a loaf cake; when mixed, make a paper case an inch wide and deep, and three or four inches long; oil it; press the paste into it, and when firm turn it out and cut into cubes. Or, instead of walnuts, use chopped almonds, flavor with vanilla, and leave the *fondant* white. This makes VANILLA ALMOND CREAM.

TUTTI FRUTTI CANDY.—Chop some almonds, citron, a *few* currants, and seedless raisins; work into some *fondant,* flavor with rum and lemon, thus making Roman punch, or with vanilla or raspberry; press into the paper forms as you did the walnut cream. You see how you can ring the changes on these bars, varying the flavoring, inventing new combinations, etc.

FONDANT PANACHÉ.—Take your *fondant*, divide it in three equal parts, color one pink and flavor as you choose, leave the other white and flavor also as you please; but it must agree with the pink, and both must agree with the next, which is chocolate. Melt a little unsweetened chocolate by setting it in a saucer over the boiling kettle, then take enough of it to make your third piece of *fondant* a fine brown; now divide the white into two parts; make each an inch and a half wide, and as long as it will; do the same with the chocolate *fondant*; then take the pink, make it the same width and length, but of course, not being divided, it will be twice as thick; now butter slightly the back of a plate, or, better still, get a few sheets of waxed paper from the confectioner's; lay one strip of the chocolate on it, then a strip of white on that, then the pink, the other white, and lastly the chocolate again; then lightly press them to make them adhere, but not to squeeze them out of shape. You have now an oblong brick of parti-colored candy; leave it for a few hours to harden, then trim it neatly with a knife and cut it crosswise into slices half an inch think, lay on waxed paper to dry, turning once in a while, and pack away in boxes.

If your *fondant* gets very hard while you work, stand it over hot water a few minutes.

Creamed candies are very fashionable just now, and, your *fondant* once ready, are very easy to make.

CREAM WALNUTS.—Make ready some almonds, some walnuts in halves, some hazelnuts, or anything of the sort you fancy; let them be very dry. Take *fondant* made from a pound of sugar, set it in a bowl in a saucepan of boiling water, stirring it till it is like cream. Then having flavored it with vanilla or lemon, drop in your nuts one by one, taking them out with the other hand on the end of a fork, resting it on the edge of your bowl to drain for a second, then drop the nut on to a waxed or buttered paper neatly. If the nut shows through the cream it is too hot; take it out of the boiling water and beat till it is just thick enough to mask the nut entirely, then return it to the boiling water, as it cools very rapidly and becomes unmanageable, when it has to be warmed over again.

VERY FINE CHOCOLATE CREAMS are made as follows: Boil half a pound of sugar with three tablespoonfuls of thick cream till it makes a *soft* ball in water, then let it cool. When cool beat it till it is very white, flavor with a few drops of vanilla and make it into balls the size of a large pea; then take some unsweetened chocolate warmed, mix it with a piece of *fondant* melted—there should be more chocolate than sugar—and when quite smooth and thick enough to mask the cream, drop them in from the end of a fork, take them out, and drop on to wax paper.

Another very fine candy to be made without heat, and therefore convenient for hot weather, is made as follows:

PUNCH DROPS.—Sift some powdered sugar. Have ready some fine white gum-arabic, put a tablespoonful with the sugar (say half a pound of sugar), and make it into a firm paste; if too wet, add more sugar, flavor with lemon and a tiny speck of tartaric acid or a very little lemon juice. Make the paste into small balls, then take more sugar and make it into icing with a spoonful of Santa Cruz rum and half the white of an egg. Try if it hardens, if not, beat in more sugar and color it a bright pink, then dip each ball in the pink icing and harden on wax paper. These are very novel, beautiful to look at, and the flavors may vary to taste.

TO MAKE COCHINEAL COLORING WHICH IS QUITE HARMLESS.—Take one ounce of powdered cochineal, one ounce of cream of tartar, two drachms of alum, half a pint of water; boil the cochineal, water, and cream of tartar till reduced to one half, then add the alum, and put up in small bottles for use. Yellow is obtained by the infusion of Spanish saffron in a little water, or a still better one from the grated rind of a ripe orange put into muslin, and a little of the juice squeezed through it.

Be careful in boiling the sugar for *fondant*, not to stir it after it is dissolved; stirring causes it to become rough instead of creamy.

CHAPTER XIV.

A CHAPTER FOR PEOPLE OF VERY SMALL MEANS.

I AM sorry to say in these days this chapter may appeal to many, who are yet not to be called "poor people," who may have been well-to-do and only suffering from the pressure of the times, and for whose cultivated appetites the coarse, substantial food of the laboring man (even if they could buy it) would not be eatable, who must have what they do have good, or starve. But, as some of the things for which I give recipes will seem over-economical for people who can afford to buy meat at least once a day, I advise those who have even fifty dollars a month income to skip it; reminding them, if they do not, "that necessity knows no law."

A bone of soup meat can be got at a good butcher's for ten or fifteen cents, and is about the best investment, for that sum I know of, as two nourishing and savory meals, at least, for four or five persons can be got from it.

Carefully make a nice soup, with plenty of vegetables, rice, or any other thickening you like. Your bone will weigh from four to six pounds, perhaps; put it on with water according to size, and let it boil down slowly until nice and strong. If you have had any scraps of meat or bones, put them also to your soup.

When you serve it, keep back a cup of soup and a few

of the vegetables, and save the meat, from which you can make a very appetizing hash in the following way: Take the meat from the bone, chop it with some cold potatoes and the vegetables you saved from the soup. Cold stewed onions, boiled carrots or turnips, all help to make the dish savory. Chop an onion very fine, unless you have cold ones, a little parsley and thyme, if liked, and sometimes, for variety's sake, if you have it, a pinch of curry powder, not enough to make it hot or yellow, yet to impart piquancy. If you have a tiny bit of fried bacon or cold ham or cold pork, chop it with the other ingredients, mix all well, moisten with the cold soup, and, when nicely seasoned, put the hash into an iron frying-pan, in which you have a little fat made hot; pack it smoothly in, cover it with a pot-lid, and either set it in a hot oven, or leave it to brown on the stove. If there was more soup than enough to moisten the hash, put it on in a tiny saucepan, with a little brown flour made into a paste with butter, add a drop of tomato catsup, or a little stewed tomato, or anything you have for flavoring, and stir till it boils. Then turn the hash out whole on a dish, it should be brown and crisp, pour the gravy you have made round it, and serve. For a change make a pie of the hash, pouring the gravy in through a hole in the top when done.

It is not generally known that a very nice plain paste can be made with a piece of bread dough, to which you have added an egg, and some lard, dripping, or butter. The dripping is particularly nice for the hash pie, and, as you need only a piece of dough as large as an orange, you will probably have enough from the soup, if you skimmed off all the fat before putting the vegetables in (see *pot-au-feu*); work your dripping into the dough, and let it rise well, then roll as ordinary pie-crust. Potato crust is also very good for plain pies of any sort, but as there are plenty of recipes for it, I will not give one here.

One of the very best hashes I ever ate was prepared by a lady who, in better times, kept a very fine table. And she told me there were a good many cold beans in it, well mashed; and often since, when taking "travelers' hash" in an hotel, I have thought of that savory dish with regret.

Instead of making your chopped meat into hash, vary it, by rolling the same mixture into egg-shaped pieces, or flat cakes, flouring them, and frying them nicely in very hot fat; pieces of pork or bacon fried and laid round will help out the dish, and be an improvement to what is already very good.

To return once more to the soup bone. If any one of your family is fond of marrow, seal up each end of the bone with a paste made of flour and water. When done, take off the paste, and remove the marrow. Made very hot, and spread on toast, with pepper and salt, it will be a relish for some one's tea or breakfast.

In this country there is a prejudice against sheep's liver; while in England, where beef liver is looked upon as too coarse to eat (and falls to the lot of the "cats-meat man," or cat butcher), sheep's is esteemed next to calf's, and it is, in fact, more delicate than beef liver. The nicest way to cook it is in very *thin* slices (not the inch-thick pieces one often sees), each slice dipped in flour and fried in pork or bacon fat, and pork or bacon served with it. But the more economical way is to put it in a pan, dredge it with flour, pin some fat pork over it, and set it in a hot oven; when very brown take it out;

make nice brown gravy by pouring water in the pan and letting it boil on the stove, stirring it well to dissolve the glaze; pour into the dish, and serve. The heart should be stuffed with bread-crumbs, parsley, thyme, and a *little* onion, and baked separately. Or, for a change, you may chop the liver up with a few sweet herbs and a little pork (onion, or not, as you like), and some bread-crumbs. Put all together in a crock, dredge with flour, cover, and set in a slow oven for an hour and a half; then serve, with toasted bread around the dish.

It is very poor economy to buy inferior meat. One pound of fine beef has more nourishment than two of poor quality. But there is a great difference in prices of different parts of meat, and it is better management to choose the cheap part of fine beef than to buy the sirloin of a poor ox even at the same price; and, by good cooking many parts not usually chosen, and therefore sold cheaply, can be made very good. Yet you must remember, that a piece of meat at seven cents a pound, in which there is at least half fat and bone, such as brisket, etc., is less economical than solid meat at ten or twelve.

Pot roasts are very good for parts of meat not tender enough for roasting, the "cross-rib," as some butchers term it, being very good for this purpose; it is all solid meat, and being very lean, requires a little fat pork, which may be laid at the bottom of the pot; or better still, holes made in the meat and pieces of the fat drawn through, larding in a rough way, so that they cut together. A pot roast is best put on in an iron pot, without water, allowed to get finely brown on one side, then turned, and when thoroughly brown on the other a little water may be added for gravy; chop parsley or any seasoning that is preferred. Give your roast at least three hours to cook. Ox cheek, as the head is called, is very good, and should be very cheap; prepare it thus:

Clean the cheek, soak it in water six hours, and cut the meat from the bones, which break up for soup; then take the meat, cut into neat pieces, put it in an earthen crock, a layer of beef, some thin pieces of pork or bacon, some onions, carrots, and turnips, cut *thin*, or chopped fine, and sprinkled over the meat; also, some chopped parsley, a little thyme, and bay leaf, pepper and salt, and a clove to each layer; then more beef and a little pork, vegetables, and seasoning, as before. When all your meat is in pour over it, if you have it, a tumbler of hard cider and one of water, or else two of water, in which put a half gill of vinegar. If you have no tight-fitting cover to your crock, put a paste of flour and water over it to keep the steam in. Place the crock in a slow oven five or six hours, and when it is taken out remove the crust and skim. Any piece of beef cooked in this way is excellent.

Ox heart is one of the cheapest of dishes, and really remarkably nice, and it is much used by economical people abroad.

The heart should be soaked in vinegar and water three or four hours, then cut off the lobes and gristle, and stuff it with fat pork chopped, bread-crumbs, parsley, thyme, pepper, and salt; then tie it in a cloth and very slowly simmer it (large end up) for two hours; take it up, remove the cloth, and flour it, and roast it a nice brown. Lay in the pan in which it is to be roasted some fat pork to baste it. Any of this left over is excellent hashed, or, warmed in slices with a rich brown gravy, cannot be told from game. Another way is to stuff it with sage and onions. It must always be served *very hot* with hot plates and on a very hot dish.

Fore quarter of mutton is another very economical part of meat, if you get your butcher to cut it so that it may not only be economical, but really afford a choice joint. Do not then let him hack the shoulder across, but, before he does a thing to it, get him to take the shoulder out in a round plate-shaped joint, with knuckle attached; if he does this well, that is, cuts it close to the bone of the ribs, you will have a nice joint; then do not have it chopped at all; this should be roasted in the oven very nicely, and served with onion sauce or stewed onions. If onions are not liked, mashed turnips are the appropriate vegetable. This joint, to be enjoyed, must be properly carved, and that is, across the middle from the edge to the bone, the same as a leg of mutton; and like the leg, you must learn, as I cannot describe it in words, where the bone lies, then have that side nearest you and cut from the opposite side.

You have, besides this joint, another roast from the ribs, or else cut it up into chops till you come to the part under the shoulder; from this the breast should be separated and both either made into a good Irish stew, or the breast prepared alone in a way I shall describe, the neck and thin ribs being stewed or boiled.

The neck of mutton is very tender boiled and served with parsley or caper sauce; the liquor it is boiled in served as broth, with vegetables and rice, or prepared as directed in a former chapter for the broth from leg of mutton.

The mode I am about to give of preparing breast of mutton was told me by a Welsh lady of rank, at whose table I ate it (it appeared as a side dish), and who said, half laughingly, "Will you take some 'fluff'? We are very fond of it, but breast of mutton is such a despised dish I never expect any one else to like it." I took it, on my principle of trying everything, and did find it very good. This lady told me that, having of course a good deal of mutton killed on her father's estate, and the breast being always despised by the servants, she had invented a way of using it to avoid waste. Her way was this:

Set the breast of mutton on the fire whole, just covered with water in which is a little salt. When it comes to the boil draw it back and let it *simmer* three hours; then take it up and draw out the bones, and lay a forcemeat of bread-crumbs, parsley, thyme, chopped suet, salt and pepper all over it; double or roll it, skewer it, and coat it thickly with egg and bread-crumbs; then bake in a moderate oven, basting it often with nice dripping or butter; when nicely brown it is done, and eats like the tenderest lamb. It was, when I saw it, served on a bed of spinach. I like it better on a bed of stewed onions.

I now give some dishes made without meat.

RAGOUT OF CUCUMBER AND ONIONS.—Fry equal quantities of large cucumbers and onions in slices until they are a nice brown. The cucumber will brown more easily if cut up and put to drain some time before using; then flour each slice. When both are brown, pour on them a cup of water, and let them stew for half an hour; then take a good piece of butter in which you have worked a dessert-spoonful of flour (browned); add pepper, salt, and a little tomato catsup or stewed tomato. This is a rich-eating dish if nicely made, and will help out cold meat or a scant quantity of it very well. A little cold meat may be added if you have it.

ONION SOUP.—Fry six large onions cut into slices with a quarter of a pound of butter till they are of a bright brown, then well mix in a tablespoonful of flour, and pour on them rather more than a quart of water. Stew gently until the onions are quite tender, season with a spoonful of salt and a little sugar; stir in quickly a *liaison* made with the yolks of two eggs mixed with a gill of milk or cream (do not let it boil afterwards), put some toast in a tureen, and serve very hot.

PEA SOUP.—Steep some yellow split peas all night, next morning set them on to boil with two quarts of water to a pint of peas; in the water put a tiny bit of soda. In another pot put a large carrot, a turnip, an onion, and a large head of celery, all cut small and covered with water. When both peas and vegetables are tender, put them together, season with salt, pepper, and a little sugar, and let them gently stew till thick enough; then strain through a colander, rubbing the vegetables well, and return to the pot while you fry some sippets of bread a crisp brown; then stir into the soup two ounces of butter in which you have rolled a little flour.

This soup is simply delicious, and the fact of it being *maigre* will not be remembered.

POTATO SOUP is another of this good kind, for meat is scarcely required, so good is it without.

Boil some potatoes, then rub them through a colandar into two quarts of hot milk (skimmed does quite well); have some fine-chopped parsley and onion, add both with salt and pepper, stew three quarters of an hour; then stir in a large piece of butter, and beat two eggs with a little cold milk, stir in quickly, and serve with fried bread. There should be potatoes enough to make the soup as thick as cream.

Do not be prejudiced against a dish because there is no meat in it, and you think it cannot be nourishing. This chapter is not written for those with whom meat, or money, is plentiful; and if it be true that man is nourished "not by what he eats, but by what he assimilates," and, according to an American medical authority, "what is eaten with distaste is not assimilated" (Dr. Hall), it follows that an enjoyable dinner, even without meat, will be more nourishing than one forced down because it lacks savor; that potato soup will be more nourishing than potatoes and butter, with a cup of milk to drink, because more enjoyable. Yet it costs no more, for the soup can be made without the eggs if they are scarce.

Or say bread and butter and onions. They will not be very appetizing, especially if they had to be a frequent meal, yet onion soup is made from the same materials, and in France is a very favorite dish, even with those well able to put meat in it if they wished.

CHAPTER XV.

A FEW THINGS IT IS WELL TO REMEMBER.

Every housekeeper has pet "wrinkles" of her own which she thinks are especially valuable; some are known to all the world, others are new to many. So it may be with mine; but, on the chance that some few things are as new to my friends as they were to me, I jot them down without any pretense of order or regularity.

Lemons will keep fresher and better in water than any other way. Put them in a crock, cover them with water. They will in winter keep two or three months, and the peel be as fresh as the day they were put in. Take care, of course, that they do not get frosted. In summer change the water twice a week; they will keep a long time.

In grating nutmegs begin at the flower end; if you commence at the other, there will be a hole all the way through.

Tea or coffee made hot (not at all scorched), before water is added, are more fragrant and stronger. Thus, by putting three spoonfuls of tea in the pot and setting in a warm place before infusing, it will be as strong as if you make tea with four spoonfuls without warming it, and much more fragrant.

Vegetables that are strong can be made much milder

by tying a bit of bread in a clean rag and boiling it with them.

Bread dough is just as good made the day before it is used; thus, a small family can have fresh bread one day, rolls the next, by putting the dough in a cold place enveloped in a damp cloth. In winter, kept cold, yet not in danger of freezing, it will keep a week.

Celery seed takes the place of celery for soup or stews when it is scarce; parsley seed of parsley.

Green beans, gherkins, etc., put down when plentiful in layers of rock salt, will keep crisp and green for months, and can be taken out and pickled when convenient.

Lemon or orange peel grated and mixed with powdered sugar and a squeeze of its own juice (the sugar making it into paste) is excellent to keep for flavoring; put it into a little pot and it will keep for a year.

Bread that is very stale may be made quite fresh for an hour or two by dipping it quickly into milk or water, and putting it in a brisk oven till *quite hot through.* It must be eaten at once, or it will be as stale as ever when cold.

Meat to be kept in warm weather should be rubbed over with salad oil, every crevice filled with ginger; meat that is for roasting or frying is much better preserved in this way than with salt; take care that every part of the surface has a coat of oil. Steaks or chops cut off, which always keep badly, should be dipped into warm butter or even dripping, if oil is not handy (the object being to exclude the air), and then hung up till wanted.

Mutton in cold weather should be hung four or five weeks in a place not subject to changes of temperature, and before it is so hung, every crevice filled with ginger and thoroughly dredged with flour, which must be then rubbed in with the hand till the surface is quite dry. This is the English fashion of keeping venison.

It may be useful for those who burn kerosene to know that when their lamps smell, give a bad light, and smoke, it is not necessary to buy new burners. Put the old ones in an old saucepan with water and a tablespoonful of soda, let them boil half an hour, wipe them, and your trouble will be over.

Meat that has become slightly tainted may be quite restored by washing it in water in which is a teaspoonful of borax, cutting away every part in the least discolored.

In summer when meat comes from the butcher's, if it is not going to be used the same day, it should be washed over with vinegar.

Poultry in summer should always have a piece of charcoal tied in a rag placed in the stomach, to be removed before cooking. Pieces of charcoal should also be put in the refrigerator and changed often.

Oyster shells put one at a time in a stove that is "clinkered" will clean the bricks entirely. They should be put in when the fire is burning brightly.

Salt and soapstone powder (to be bought at the druggist's) mend fire brick; use equal quantities, make into a paste with water, and cement the brick; they will be as strong as new ones.

Ink spilled on carpets may be entirely removed by rubbing while wet with blotting paper, using fresh as it soils.

CHAPTER XVI.

ON SOME TABLE PREJUDICES.

MANY people have strong prejudices against certain things which they have never even tasted, or which they do frequently take and like as a part of something else, without knowing it. How common it is to hear and see untraveled people declare that they dislike garlic, and could not touch anything with it in. Yet those very people will take Worcestershire sauce, in which garlic is actually predominant, with everything they eat; and think none but English pickles eatable, which owe much of their excellence to the introduction of a *soupçon* of garlic. Therefore I beg those who actually only know garlic from hearsay abuse of it, or from its presence on the breath of some inveterate garlic eater, to give it a fair trial when it appears in a recipe. It is just one of those things that require the most delicate handling, for which the French term a "*suspicion*" is most appreciated; it should only be a suspicion, its presence should never be pronounced. As Blot once begged his readers, "Give garlic a fair trial in a *rémolade* sauce." (Montpellier butter beaten into mayonnaise is a good *rémolade* for cold meat or fish.)

Curry is one of those things against which many are strongly prejudiced, and I am inclined to think it is quite an acquired taste, but a taste which is an enviable one to its possessors; for them there is endless variety in all they eat. The capabilities of curry are very little known in this country, and, as the taste for it is so limited, I will not do more in its defense than indicate a pleasant use to which it may be put, and in which form it would be a welcome condiment to many to whom "a curry," pure and simple, would be obnoxious. I once knew an Anglo-Indian who used curry as most people use cayenne; it was put in a pepper-box, and with it he would at times pepper his fish or kidneys, even his eggs. Used in this way, it imparts a delightful piquancy to food, and is neither hot nor " spicy."

Few people are so prejudiced as the English generally, and the stay-at-home Americans; but the latter are to be taught by travel, the Englishman rarely.

The average Briton leaves his island shores with the conviction that he will get nothing fit to eat till he gets back, and that he will have to be uncommonly careful once across the channel, or he will be having fricasseed frogs palmed on him for chicken. Poor man! in his horror of frogs, he does not know that the Paris restaurateur who should give the costly frog for chicken, would soon end in the bankruptcy court.

"If I could only get a decent dinner, a good roast and plain potato, I would like Paris much better," said an old Englishman to me once in that gay city.

"But surely you can."

"No; I have been to restaurants of every class, and called for beefsteak and roast beef, but have never got the real article, although it's my belief," said he, leaning forward solemnly, "that I have eaten *horse* three times this week." Of course the Englishman of rank, who has spent half his life on the continent, is not at all the *average* Englishman.

Americans think the hare and rabbits, of which the English make such good use, very mean food indeed, and if they are unprejudiced enough to try them, from the fact that they are never well cooked, they dislike them, which prejudice the English reciprocate by looking on squirrels as being as little fit for food as a rat. And a familiar instance of prejudice from ignorance carried even to insanity, is that of the Irish in 1848, starving rather than eat the "yaller male," sent them by generous American sympathizers; yet they come here and soon get over that dislike. Not so the French, who look on oatmeal and Indian meal as most unwholesome food. "*Ça pèse sur l'estomac, ça creuse l'estomac*," I heard an old Frenchwoman say, trying to dissuade a mother from giving her children mush.

The moral of all of which is, that for our comfort's sake, and the general good we should avoid unreasonable prejudices against unfamiliar food. We of course have a right to our honest dislikes; but to condemn things because we have heard them despised, is prejudice.

CHAPTER XVII.

A CHAPTER OF ODDS AND ENDS.

I HAVE alluded, in an earlier chapter, to the fact that many inexperienced cooks are afraid of altering recipes; a few words on this subject may not be out of place. As a rule, a recipe should be faithfully followed in all important points; for instance, in making soup you cannot, because you are short of the given quantity of meat, put the same amount of water as directed for the full quantity, without damaging your soup; but you may easily reduce water and *every other ingredient* in the same proportion; and, in mere matters of flavoring, you may vary to suit circumstances. If you are told to use cloves, and have none, a bit of mace may be substituted.

If you read a recipe, and it calls for something you have not, consider whether that something has anything to do with the substance of the dish, or whether it is merely an accessory for which something else can be substituted. For instance, if you are ordered to use cream in a sauce, milk with a larger amount of well-washed butter may take its place; but if you are told to use cream for charlotte russe or trifles, there is no way in which you could make milk serve, since it is not an accessory but the chief part of those dishes. For a cake in which cream is used, butter whipped to a cream may take its place. Wine is usually optional in savory dishes; it gives richness only.

Again, in cakes be very careful the exact proportions of flour, eggs, and milk are observed; of butter you can generally use more or less, having a more or less rich cake in proportion. In any but plain cup cakes (which greatly depend on soda and acid for their lightness) never lessen the allowance of eggs; never add milk if a cake is too stiff (but an extra egg may always be used), unless milk is ordered in the recipe, when more or less may be used as needed. Flavoring may be always varied.

In reducing a recipe always reduce *every ingredient*, and it can make no difference in the results. Sometimes, in cookery books, you are told to use articles not frequently found in ordinary kitchens; for instance, a larding-needle (although that can be bought for twenty-five cents at any house-furnishing store, and should always be in a kitchen); but, in case you have not one for meat, you may manage by making small cuts and inserting slips of bacon.

Another article that is very useful, but seldom, if ever, to be found in small kitchens, is a salamander; but when you wish to brown the top of a dish, and putting it in the oven would not do, or the oven is not quick enough to serve, an iron shovel, made nearly red, and a few red cinders in it, is a very good salamander. It must be held over the article that requires browning near enough to color it, yet not to burn.

In the recipes I have given nothing is required that cannot be obtained, with more or less ease, in New York. For syrups, fruit juices, etc., apply to your druggist; if he has not them he will tell you where to obtain them. We often make up our minds that because a thing is not commonly used in this country, it is impossible to get it. Really there are very few things not to be got in New

York City to the intelligent seeker. You need an article of French or Italian or may be English grocery, that your grocer, a first-class one, perhaps, has not, and you make up your mind you cannot get it. But go into the quarters where French people live, and you can get everything belonging to the French *cuisine*. So prejudiced are the French in favor of the productions of *la belle France*, that they do not believe in our parsley or our chives or garlic or shallots; for I know at least one French grocer who imports them for his customers. On being asked why he brought them from France to a country where those very things were plentiful, he answered :

"Oh, French herbs are much finer."

Needless to say tarragon is one of the herbs so imported, and can thus be bought; but, as several New Jersey truck gardeners grow all kinds of French herbs, they can be got in Washington Market, and most druggists keep them dried; but for salads, Montpellier butter, and some other uses, the dried herb would not do, although for flavoring it would serve; but the far better way is to grow them for yourself, as I have done. Any large seedsman will supply you with burnet, tarragon, and borage (very useful for salads, punch, etc.) seeds, and if you live in the country, have an herb bed; if in town, there are few houses where there is not ground enough to serve for the purpose; but even in these few houses one can have a box of earth in the kitchen window, in which your seeds will flourish.

Parsley is a thing in almost daily request in winter, yet it is very expensive to buy it constantly for the sake of using the small spray that often suffices. It is a good plan, therefore, in fall, to get a few roots, plant them in a pot or box, and they will flourish all winter, if kept where they will not freeze, and be ready for garnishing at any minute.

Always, as far as your means allow, have every convenience for cooking. By having utensils proper for every purpose you save a great deal of work and much vexation of spirit. Yet it should be no excuse for bad work that such utensils are not at hand. A willing and intelligent cook will make the best of what she has. Apropos of this very thing Gouffé relates that a friend of his, an "artist" of renown, was sent for to the chateau of a Baron Argenteuil, who had taken a large company with him, unexpectedly crowding the chateau in every part. He was shown into a dark passage in which a plank was suspended from the ceiling, and told this was to be his kitchen. He had to fashion his own utensils, for there was nothing provided, and his pastry he had to bake in a frying-pan—besides building two monumental *pláts* on that board—and prepare a cold *entrée*. But he cheerfully set to work to overcome difficulties, achieved his task, and was rewarded by the plaudits of the diners. Such difficulties as these our servants never have to encounter, and a cheerful endeavor to make the best of everything should be the rule. Yet, let us spare them all the labor we can, or rather make it as easy and pleasant as possible; they will be more proud of their well-furnished kitchen, more cheerful in it, than they will of one where everything for their convenience is grudged, and such pride and cheerfulness will be your gain.

There is always a great deal of talk about servants in America, how bad and inefficient they are, how badly they contrast with those of England. Certainly, they are not so efficient as those of the older country; how could they be? There, girls who are intended for servants have ever held before their eyes what they may or may not do in the future calling, and how it is to be done. But take one of these orderly, efficient girls, put her in an American family as general servant or as cook, where two are kept, washing and ironing to do, and a variety of other work, and see how your English servant would stare at your requirements. She has been accustomed to her own line of work at home; if housemaid, she has been dressed for the day at noon; if cook, she has never done even her own washing.

She may, and will no doubt, fall into the way of the country, after a while, and on account of her early habits of respect, will make a good servant perhaps. But many of them would be quite indignant at being asked to do the average servant's work here. I am speaking now of the *trained* servants; but, comparing the London "maid-of-all-work" or "slavey" with our own general servants, and considering how much more is expected of the latter, the comparison seems to me vastly in the favor of our own Bridgets. We may rest assured, however smoothly the wheels of household management glide along in wealthy families across the water, people who can only keep one or two have all our troubles with servants and a few added, and their faults are just as general a subject of conversation among ladies.

France (out of Paris, from Parisian servants deliver me!) and Germany seem the favored lands where one servant does the work of three or four. Yet even they, are, they say, degenerating. Let us, then, be contented and make the best of what we have, assured that even Biddy is not so hopeless as she is painted. Kindness (not weakness), firmness, and patience work wonders, even with the roughest Emerald that ever crossed the sea.

I have said somewhere else that you must beware of attempting too much at once; perfect yourself in one thing before you attempt another. Take breaded chops or fried oysters, make opportunities for having them rather often, and do not rest satisfied until you have them as well fried as you have ever seen them anywhere; "practice makes perfect," and you certainly will achieve perfection if you are not discouraged by one failure. But above all things never make experiments for company; let them be made when it really matters little whether you succeed or not, and let your experiments be on a *small* scale; don't attempt to fry a *large* dish of oysters or chops until it is a very easy task, or make more than half a pound of puff paste at first; for if you fail with a large task before you, you will be tired and disheartened, hate the sight of what you are doing, and, as a consequence, not be likely to return to it very soon. The same may be said of cooks; some of them are very fond of experiments, which taste I should always encourage; but do not let them jump from one experiment to the other; if they try a dish and fail, they often make up their minds that the fault is not theirs, that it is not worth while to "bother" with it. Here your knowledge will be of service; you will show them that it can be done, how it should be done, and order the dish cook failed in, frequently, giving it sufficient surveillance to prevent your family suffering from her inexperience; for, as a witty Frenchman said of Mme. du Deffaud's cook, "Between her and Brinvilliers there is only the difference of intention."

Few things add more to a man or woman's social reputation than the fact that they keep a good table. It need not be one where

> "The strong table groans
> Beneath the smoking sirloin stretched immense;"

but a table where whatever you do have will be good, be it pork and beans, or salmi; the pork and beans would satisfy a Bostonian, the salmi Grimod de la Reynière himself. I do not admit with Di Walcott that

> "The turnpike road to people's hearts I find
> Lies through their mouths, or I mistake mankind."

But it is a fact that good living—by this I do not mean extravagant living—presupposes good breeding. Well-bred people sometimes live badly; but ill-bred people seldom or ever live well, in the right sense of the term.

Now, by way of valedictory, let me repeat that I do not think a lady's best or proper place is the kitchen; but it is quite possible to have a perfectly served table, yet spend very little time there. Only that one little hour a day that Talleyrand, the busy man full of intrigue and statecraft, found time to spend with his cook, would insure your table being well served. For, after devoting say a few winter months to perfecting yourself in a few things, you will be able to teach your cook, who is often ambitious to excel if put in the right way. A word here about cooks.

The knowledge that if they fail to do a thing well you will do it yourself, will often put them on their mettle to do their best; while the feeling that you don't know, will make them careless.

Servants have a great deal more *amour propre* than people imagine; therefore, stimulate it by judicious praise and appreciation; let them think that to send in a dish perfect, is a glory to themselves as well as a pleasure to you. While careful to remark when alone with them upon any fault that results from carelessness, be equally careful to give all the praise you can, and repeat to them complimentary remarks that may have been made on their skill. Servants are usually—such is the weakness of feminine nature, whether in the drawing-room or the kitchen—very sensitive to the praise or blame of the gentlemen of the family. Indulge poor humanity a little when you honestly can.

PART II.

PRACTICAL RECIPES.

CHAPTER XVIII.

BREAKFAST BREADS.

ALTHOUGH breads were very fully treated of in the first part of this book, a few breakfast and tea-cakes more quickly made may not be out of place.

SOUFFLEE ROLLS.

Melt a tablespoonful of butter in half a pint of milk; when blood-warm put in half a cake of compressed yeast, a beaten egg, two teaspoonfuls of sugar and a saltspoonful of salt. When the yeast is dissolved, stir in a cup and a-half of flour well dried and quite warm; beat two or three minutes; it should be too thick for batter, and not thick enough for dough—so thick that you cannot take it up in a spoon at all; cover with a hot cloth, and set it in a warm place; it will rise in about two hours; if you have time, the texture will be better if you beat it down and let it rise again before putting it in the tins. They will be very good, however, if you simply stir it down well, and with a tablespoon dipped in flour, fill small roll-pans with the batter rather more than half full; let them rise till the pans are full, and then bake ten to fifteen minutes in a very quick oven; when pale-brown brush them over with a little syrup thinned with milk, and bake till quite brown; be careful they do not burn—the syrup causes them to do so easily.

SCOTCH SCONES.

Dissolve half a saltspoonful of soda and two ounces of butter or lard in a gill of warmed sour milk; put ten ounces of flour and a little salt in a bowl; pour the mixture in and make it into a stiff dough; roll it out into a round cake half an inch thick; mark it in eight sections and bake on a griddle fifteen to twenty minutes; split and butter while hot.

SCONES NO. 2.

Melt in half a pint of milk one ounce of butter; beat up an egg and stir it into the milk; with a saltspoonful of salt add enough fine flour mixed with a teaspoonful of baking powder to make a very *soft* dough; flour the board thickly and make into round cakes, the size of a small plate, an inch thick; mark into sections and bake twenty minutes on a griddle; split and butter while hot.

CORN BREAD.

One quart of milk, three eggs, two cups of Indian meal, three cups of flour, one teaspoonful of soda, two of cream of tartar, lard half the size of an egg, one level teaspoon of salt; mix Indian meal and flour; sift cream of tartar to them; stir with the milk into a smooth batter; beat the yolks of the eggs; stir them in; melt the lard and add it; then beat the whites to a stiff foam and stir them in; dissolve the soda in very little boiling water, and add it last thing; bake in a very quick oven.

CORN MUFFINS.

One cup of corn-meal, one of flour, a dessert-spoonful of butter, two eggs, two small teaspoonfuls of baking-powder, one tablespoonful of sugar.

Mix flour and meal and sugar with enough milk to make a stiff batter; beat the eggs, melt the butter, and add them to it; stir in the baking-powder with a small teaspoonful of salt.

EGG BISCUITS.

Sift with one pint of flour one teaspoonful of baking-powder; chop into it a tablespoonful of butter till fine; beat one egg and mix it with half a cup of milk—part cream is much better; make a hole in the flour; put in a saltspoonful of salt, and pour in the egg and milk; mix altogether into a *soft* dough, using more milk if needful; roll out as quickly as possible half an inch thick; cut into rounds and bake in a quick oven.

BATTER BREAD.

Two eggs, the whites beaten separately, a small cup of flour, the same of milk; mix yolks, flour and milk into a smooth batter; stir in a tablespoonful of butter melted and a little salt; then add the whites of the eggs beaten till they stand high, and a teaspoonful of baking-powder; mix gently after the whites are in; bake in a well-buttered tin in a *very* hot oven.

ENGLISH MUFFINS.

Dissolve a yeast-cake (compressed) in a pint of warm water, with a teaspoonful of salt ; mix with as much warmed flour as will make a very thick batter—just as thick as can be stirred without being dough; set to rise, and when like a honeycomb, it is ready; *flour* the griddle, which must be moderately hot ; sprinkle some flour in a saucer ; take with tablespoon dipped into flour a piece of the dough as large as a croquet ball ; drop it in the saucer ; swing it round in it till it forms a round mass, and drop it on the griddle; do the others the same way; do not turn them till they look almost cooked through, then brown them on the other side.

English muffins are never baked in rings, yet if rings were made three and a half inches in diameter it would save much trouble, for they are too soft to handle, and it requires knack and practice to shape them really well with the saucer.

They are better made the day before they are to be eaten; they should be split a little all round, then toasted on both sides quite crisp ; rip them open quickly and don't attempt to spread butter on them, but lay it in little bits all over each piece ; put them together again; butter the outside, and cut them once across and set them in the oven for the butter to melt ; if you have eaten them this way, you will not be satisfied with having them merely made hot in the oven.

QUICK BISCUIT.

Chop a tablespoonful of butter or lard in two heaping cups of flour in which you have sifted a teaspoonful of baking-powder, and half one of salt; wet with milk or water enough to make a soft dough that you can just roll out; roll it out half an inch thick and cut with a cutter into round cakes.

BUTTERMILK PUFFS.

To a quart of sharp buttermilk put half a teaspoonful of baking-soda; taste; if not sweet add a little more; stir into it a teaspoonful of salt, one of sugar, and enough flour to make a thick batter that will drop in lumps from a spoon; mix it all up very quickly, then drop on a buttered baking-pan in little mounds.

These require a very hot oven, and will bake in seven minutes. If your buttermilk is not rich, rub a little butter into the flour till it is like sand; these should only take about twelve minutes from the time you begin them till they are out of the oven; they are delicious.

CHAPTER XIX.

OMELETTES.

FRENCH OMELETTE.

Break four eggs; beat them, but not very much, just so that you can take them up without strings; put a piece of butter in a very clean smooth frying-pan and let it get hot but not burn; put a saltspoonful of salt in the eggs, and pour them in the pan; as the egg sets, shift it from the sides with a spoon that the uncooked part may run in its place; do not let it quite set; fold it half over; shake the pan and slip the omelette off on to a dish.

This is the true French omelette. It has one drawback, it must be eaten *at once* or it will be tough and heavy. The addition of a little milk—a tablespoonful to two eggs—tends to prevent it getting tough so quickly. Neither of these omelettes can be kept, not even for a minute, and for that reason where you are not sure of your cook, and do not want to make the dish with your own hands, I recommend the one mentioned on page 45. It is good till cold and always handsome, yet true omelette lovers would not approve of it.

Any kind of savory omelette is but a variation on this plain one.

TOMATO OMELETTE, (TWO WAYS).

Make some good tomato sauce—see recipe—very hot, pour it in the dish round the omelette.

Or, Make some stewed tomato hot; lay two tablespoonfuls of it on the omelette before you double it over.

OYSTER OMELETTE.

Fricassee some oysters as for oyster patties; lay them on the omelette before folding it.

MUSHROOM OMELETTE.

Use stewed mushrooms as directed for oysters and tomatoes.

HAM OMELETTE.

May have a little *cooked* ham chopped and put in before frying, or delicately shaved cold ham may be made hot and laid between the omelette.

In short, there are innumerable ways of varying omelettes which it would be mere repetition to give here.

CHAPTER XX.

GENERAL INSTRUCTIONS.

CARAMEL FOR COLORING.

Put four tablespoonfuls of sugar in a small thick saucepan, with two tablespoonfuls of water; let them boil ten minutes over a quick fire; then watch it till it colors golden; it will soon go from this to dark-brown; when it is *all black* like thick molasses, put a half cup of hot water to it; it will sputter, but never mind that; stir till it is all dissolved; then let it boil till it is syrup; pour it into a bottle; it should look when cold like black molasses and will keep for years.

BOUQUET OF SWEET HERBS.

Tie together two sprigs of parsley, one of thyme, one bay leaf, wrapping them round so that they will not shed, and be easy to take out of the gravy or soup.

TO CHOP HERBS.

Always use the leaves only, never the stems; gather the leaves firmly between the thumb and three fingers of the left hand; let a sharp knife shave them through as you push them forward under it; turn them round; gather them up again and cut them across in the same way; then finish by chopping with both hands.

THIS IS THE WAY TO GET THEM FINELY AND EVENLY CHOPPED. When sweet herbs are called for, it means three parts parsley, two parts thyme, one part marjoram.

GARNISHING.

No matter how well a dinner may be cooked if it is ill served it will lose a great deal. Everybody should insist on the dishes being well arranged, and trimmed or garnished before they are sent to table.

Corned beef is a very homely dish, yet if the carrots and turnips are cut into nice forms and served round it alternately, with here and there a sprig of green parsley, it will look far more appetizing than if it is on a bare dish, and so it is with most other things, from hash to croquettes.

Parsley is probably the most useful garnish we have, yet a dish garnished with parsley does not mean a kitchen-garden of it, and the tendency is usually to *overdo*. The mere fact, that you insist on the dishes being made to look their best, tends to make a cook careful in her cooking. They are impressed with the fact that the slap-dash method will not do. An Hibernian damsel applied to me for a place, and in awe-struck tones, as if it enhanced her own value to be so near the rose, told me her sister was cook to Mr. Y., who never had a dish sent to table without "Varnish." My thoughts flew to "glaze," and as it was rather an advanced form of cooking for our locality, I asked if she herself knew how to make the "Varnish." A bewildered look passed over her face, a suspicion that I was laughing at her, as she said in a tone of dignified rebuke: "It grows;" so I knew her "Varnish" was "garnish," her one idea of "garnish" parsley.

Fried parsley is suitable for any *light* brown article, such as savory patties, croquettes, cromesquis, sweetbreads, etc.; and it makes a change from the too pervasive uncooked article, pretty as it is.

For hot dishes with brown gravy, fried bread cut into pretty shapes will not take two minutes, or as they will keep a month in cool weather many may be prepared when there is leisure, and made quite hot in a slow oven. They will not be so nice, yet better than sodden toasted sippets.

White dishes such as fricassee are very nicely garnished with little ornaments of puff paste glazed with egg and baked a pale brown. Clubs, hearts, diamonds and spades cut out of carrots, beetroot, and English pickled walnuts and scattered over a white entrée makes a novel garnish. But the ways are many and open to any one's invention, only take care that the garnish suits the dish.

I am unorthodox enough to think that flowers do not suit salad unless they are the flowers of a vegetable, or salad plant, such as nasturtiums and scarlet runner blossoms, bean or pea blossoms, etc. To me flowers suggest sweet things, and are appropriate to fruit dishes.

FRIED PARSLEY.

The whole secret is in having fresh *curled* parsley, bright in color, and *perfectly dry*. It is better not washed; therefore never use any but the cleanest. Have the fat in the frying-kettle hot enough to brown a cube of bread in a few seconds; put the parsley in a frying-basket; put it in the fat, and in *half a minute*, if the fat is hot enough, it will be crisp and green; it will break easily when you take it out; lay it on blotting-paper or grocer's tea-paper to absorb the grease.

CROUTONS, which sound very fine, are just pieces of stale bread cut with a cutter into pretty shapes and dropped into the same hot fat; they will take one minute to become golden brown; never let them be a dark color. Nicely-made hash served on the centre of small rounds of fried bread, with a little parsley, becomes an entrée instead of a make-shift dish.

EGGS carefully broken and dropped into this same kettle of boiling fat, and laid round a dish of nice hash, make a very different breakfast-dish to one of hash with boiled eggs, yet the expense is the same and the trouble no more. Once you get used to using the deep frying-kettle, it will be so much easier than the sauté—otherwise, frying-pan—that you will think nothing of using it, and turning out golden wonders even if you are in the greatest hurry. Eggs (to return to the subject) fried one minute in this way, come out golden-brown balls.

LARDING—DAUBING.

Larding is a process that requires practice, when it is very easy; it means to take a stitch in the surface of meat, and is really more ornamental than anything else. For purposes of moistening and flavoring dry meats, the process called "daubing" is far better and perfectly easy.

In larding cut the strips of solid salt pork about the third of an inch square and two inches long for large pieces of meat, a quarter of an inch for smaller, and as thick as a good straw for poultry. Cut the strips, which are called *lardoons*, parallel to the rind some time before you want them, and lay them on ice; take care they are never too large for the needle. Mark the surface of the meat at equal distances with a knife, then put in the larding-needle at the first mark; push it almost up to the end, bringing the point out at the second mark, then pull it back, insert the lardoon in it, and bring it through, leaving the pork in the meat and an end where it entered and where it came out.

Meat *à la daube* has holes made through it and pieces of pork as thick as your finger inserted; they go all through the meat.

TO CRUMB.

Where you have not a large quantity of ready dried and sifted bread-crumbs it is better to use the cracker powder that comes in boxes. It is just as economical to turn out a whole box when you are crumbing, for what is not used is sifted and returned to the box.

To crumb croquettes, cutlets, etc., beat up one or two eggs (according as you have many or few articles) with a teaspoon of oil and one of water and a little salt, or the water may be used alone.

Have the egg in a saucer, and articles to be crumbed on your right, and the cracker meal on your left, a dish covered with cracker meal within reach. Dip each article with the right hand in the egg, lay it on the cracker meal with the left, roll it well in it and lay it on the dish; do not wet the left hand in the egg at all.

CHAPTER XXI.

FORCEMEATS.—STUFFING.

FORCEMEATS.

Many people believe they don't like dishes flavored with herbs; yet they dine and enjoy dinner where herbs are *properly* used, and never know the dish they enjoyed owed its piquancy to their despised "yarbs." Herbs in the hands of an inexperienced or careless person are dangerous things—so are spices, and most of the prejudice comes from their association with bad cooking.

Any attempt to make good forcemeat without herbs degenerates into making the first stage of a bread-pudding, and omitting everything that makes it good.

Yet one remedy there is for those who do not want wet bread with an onion flavor, yet really cannot eat herbs, and that is in sausage-meat. Really good sausage-meat put into the *breast* of a turkey or chicken is a great improvement to the bird: its richness moistens it and adds much to the flavor; it must not go into the body, or it becomes steamed and unpleasant.

CHESTNUT FORCEMEAT.

Peel some Spanish chestnuts; scald them a few minutes to get off the inner skin; drain them and stew them till tender in gravy; let them get cold and pound them with an equal quantity of butter and bread-crumbs, adding the latter after they are pounded; season with pepper, salt and nutmeg; bind with the yolks of two eggs.

This is used for turkey, and may be fried in balls to garnish it.

OYSTER FORCEMEAT.

Take two dozen plump oysters, scald them, chop them a little; take an equal quantity of bread-crumbs and two ounces of butter; scald a bit of onion as large as a hazel-nut, and chop it very fine; put in a teaspoonful of finely-chopped parsley, a small saltspoonful of pepper, and two of salt (it must be highly seasoned); squeeze in the juice of half a lemon, and bind the whole with the yolks of two eggs; used for turkey, roasted or boiled, or may be fried in balls to garnish.

SAGE AND ONION FORCEMEAT,

for ducks, pork and goose.

Boil some white onions till half done; chop them fine; put as much bread-crumbs as there is chopped onion, and to about a pint of stuffing put about ten sage-leaves, dried till they powder easily. Season with salt and pepper, highly.

ORDINARY VEAL-STUFFING—(SOYER'S).

Chop up half a pound of beef suet very fine (I substitute butter—four ounces); put it in a bowl with eight ounces of bread-crumbs, two tablespoonfuls of finely-chopped parsley, two teaspoonfuls of equal quantities of powdered thyme and marjoram, a suspicion of lemon-peel grated, and the juice of half a lemon, a quarter of a nutmeg, and a teaspoonful of salt; one-sixth of one of pepper; bind with two yolks of eggs.

This is suitable for turkey, chickens, or baked fish.

HOW TO STUFF.

In stuffing any bird, fish, or piece of meat, avoid packing it tightly—there must be room for the stuffing to swell; beside, the stuffing should be well permeated with the gravy of the article. Turkeys and chickens should be stuffed in the breast, loosening the skin with the finger; geese and ducks in the stomach. No more should be put in the latter than will go loosely in without any pressure, or it will come out like steamy pudding.

TO BLANCH.

French cooks mean by this term to pour boiling water on any article and then to put it immediately in cold water. With almonds it means scalding them to take off the skin.

CHAPTER XXII.

VEGETABLES.

TO BOIL VEGETABLES.

There is not much to add to what has been said in the chapter on boiling, in the first part of this book. Multiplying recipes is not adding to information; nothing is more generally spoilt than vegetables, yet the simple rules there given would prevent this, and no number of recipes would do so.

It is usually the question of time that destroys boiled vegetables; never over-cook them—never put them on too early, but each in their time. I give a general order each day (knowing the incapacity of average servants to remember differences of time unless it is fixed for them).

Put on potatoes just half an hour before dinner-time, peas or asparagus ten minutes, cabbage or cauliflower five minutes later, turnips a quarter of an hour, and carrots, in fall and early winter, half an hour before them; in winter, one hour before the potatoes; and *always* put them in boiling water; *always* make them boil up quickly again.

If you are forced to cook vegetables before they are wanted, pour them off directly they are done and throw them into cold water; when required drain them, and make them hot in the sauce you serve with them; this is the French method; it preserves color and flavor, and leaves the range free for other cooking, and is absolutely necessary when serving a dinner of many dishes.

TO CUT VEGETABLES.

Peel turnips thick; scrape carrots or peel them very thin, and cut them into slices the third of an inch thick; make three slices in a pile, and cut them across.

TO CUT AND SHRED VEGETABLES.

Prepare them as directed; cut carrots, turnips, (or onions) in slices the third of an inch thick; then make them into piles, three slices in a pile, and cut down through them every third of an inch, pushing the piles forward with the left hand as the knife comes down.

These will be about the size to boil and serve with white sauce. They need to be cut precisely, not only for the appearance, but because if they are unequal in size, some will be over-cooked and others under-done.

TO SHRED FOR SOUP

Cut the slices much thinner; five or six to the inch; hold them in little piles firmly between the left thumb and fingers, and cut across each pile evenly, making about six cuts to the inch; with a little practice this becomes the quickest way of cutting vegetables, and far more nicely than cutting them hap-hazard.

PREPARATION OF VEGETABLES.

CAULIFLOWER—Should have nearly all the green leaves trimmed off, leaving only one circle of the young green; lay in cold water to cover them, in which is a large handful of salt. Then rinse out of this in two waters. It may be tied up in an old napkin, which keeps any speck of scum from it. It should boil till the stalk is just tender, about twenty-five minutes, with a level saltspoonful of soda, and a tablespoonful of salt in the water, which should cover it well; serve with Hollandaise or white sauce; and, if liked, a little parmesan cheese may be grated over it.

CABBAGE—Is to be cooked in exactly the same manner, and unless in deep winter, will take no longer; in winter allow half an hour—but cabbage requires a *large* pot and *plenty* of water; to be frequently pushed down, and to boil without a cover as fast as possible—" to gallop" as the common phrase is. You will have then no bad odor from it. Take care the pot is large enough to prevent the water splashing over on the stove.

PEAS—Require twenty minutes boiling, unless very old, in just enough water in which a teaspoonful of sugar to each quart is dissolved, and a teaspoonful of salt; serve with plain butter in the dish.

STRING BEANS.

To look well, these should be most carefully cut slant-wise, in thin uniform slices; or if very young, slit them the whole length, and cut across twice to make slips an inch long, like those that come in the French tins.

They should never be chopped across, any size from half an inch to an inch, as careless cooks so often do. They take twenty to twenty-five minutes in well salted fast boiling water in which is half a saltspoon of soda; serve either with plain butter or *thin* drawn butter in which is a mere suspicion of sugar.

ASPARAGUS—Must be scraped; cut about an even five inches long; tied in small bundles and boiled *gently* in well salted water; standing, if possible, as you thus save the heads; they take twenty minutes, and are served with white sauce or Hollandaise.

CARROTS—Should be scraped, not peeled; split if large, and cut in four (if to eat with boiled beef), and boiled one hour and a half. If they are to be served separate, cut them in slips, (see Cutting Vegetables) and boiled one hour in salted water; they may then be dressed with butter or white sauce.

CONES OF CARROT AND TURNIPS.

A more ornamental way is to boil them in quarters; chop them fine in a chopping-bowl; put a piece of butter with them and press them into a cone shape (a conical wineglass will answer for a mould), and stand them in a dish; sprinkle over them dry-chopped parsley.

When carrots and white turnips are both served, mash the turnips and press them in the same way, arranging the orange and white cones alternately on the dish; garnish with parslay.

TURNIPS should be *thickly* peeled, cut in halves, and boiled one hour in well-salted water; they are usually tender in that time. If you wish to mash them, pour off the water; mash them with a tablespoonful of cream and half a saltspoonful of white pepper; salt to taste; a *little* butter may be used instead of cream, but the flavor of butter should not be very perceptible.

A better way to cook them is to cut them (see Cutting Vegetables) and boil forty-five minutes in salted water, then served with white sauce.

Young spring turnips and carrots require less time to boil, according to size, and should be served whole and be simply dressed with white sauce.

SPINACH requires careful washing to free it from sand; pick off all discolored leaves and cut off the roots.

I always boil it *without* water twenty minutes or till tender, *leaving the cover on* the saucepan; when done, there will be perhaps half a pint of water in the saucepan after the spinach is taken out; chop the spinach fine in a chopping-bowl; put butter, the size of an egg, and a teaspoonful of flour in it and salt and pepper to taste; return it to the saucepan and let it stew till all the water has boiled away, stirring *often* to prevent it burning.

The usual way, however, is to put it in boiling water with only a little salt; let it boil twenty minutes; pour off the water and chop the spinach, as in last recipe.

SWEET CORN should not be stripped of the husk until just before using; put it into boiling water; boil twenty minutes, and serve in a hot napkin.

Many prefer to boil it in the husk, and to strip it before sending it to table.

TOMATOES, STEWED.—Scald them to remove the skin; cut them up; put them in a saucepan, and let them stew down slowly till they are thick from one to two hours; put in a lump of butter, pepper and salt, and a teaspoonful of flour; let them stew five minutes longer and serve.

TOMATOES, BAKED.—Scald them; skin them; cut a hole in the top and put in it a little knob of butter in which you have worked a quarter saltspoonful of salt and a little pepper; set them in a dripping-pan; put in it butter the size of an egg, and two teaspoonfuls of flour kneaded in it; bake them till tender and brown, but not till they are all shrunken away; take them up and set the pan on the stove; stir the juice well, which the lump of butter and flour will have served to thicken; when smooth, put it to the tomatoes and serve.

ONIONS, STEWED.—Take care that the onions are carefully peeled; it is better to take off a skin too much than leave one that will shrivel; choose them of medium size; let them boil quite tender in well salted water—they will take about an hour if not large—and serve with white sauce or drawn butter.

SPRING ONIONS, trimmed to leave about two inches of the green (making them four or five inches long), boiled about twenty-five minutes, and served as you would asparagus, are a delicate and delicious dish.

CHAPTER XXIII.

SOUPS.

CLEAR SOUP.—For beef stock, for all clear soups, I can do no better than refer to the minute directions for the making of Gouffe's Pot-au-feu, given on page 68. That stock, carefully prepared, clear as follows :

To each quart of stock take the white and shell of one egg, to which add a wineglass of cold water; then beat well together; add a little of the boiling stock *gradually*, still beating the egg; then stir the stock quickly and pour in the white of egg, etc., at the same time stirring till nearly boiling again; then take it from the fire, let it stand a few minutes that the white of egg may separate from the soup into a curd; then pour through a clean, fine cloth or napkin into a bowl.

You now have a soup nearly colorless, clear as water, and of delicious flavor. Add to it one-half teaspoonful of caramel (see recipe), or less, and it becomes like *pale* sherry or *weak* tea. This is the ideal clear soup or bouillon. Had you reduced it before clearing, by quick boiling, from two quarts to one (see page 67), you would have *consommée*, and then the color may be made a very little darker. Avoid a dark color, however, either for bouillon or *consommée*.

VERMICELLI SOUP.—To one quart of clear soup or bouillon, add two ounces of vermicelli; boil gently ten minutes and serve.

CLEAR VEGETABLE SOUP.—Shred half a small carrot, half a small turnip, about an inch of young leek or half a dozen very small spring onions, if in season; also a few green peas or string beans *if young;* boil all together till quite tender, in salted water; then add them, just before serving, to the clear, hot stock. Take care that you have all the vegetables of one size, or some will cook to mash while others are hard; they should be not more than an inch in length and the thickness of a match. To a quart there should not be more added than two tablespoonfuls altogether, each in good proportion. In winter, canned peas and beans can be used.

CONSOMMÉE À LA ROYALE.—For two quarts of consommée, take the yolks of two eggs and one gill of the consommée; beat the eggs; mix with the gill of consommée; put as much grated nutmeg as will lie on the point of a penknife and a small pinch of salt; pour this custard into a cup; set it in hot water, cover it, and bake till firm, not longer. When done, if there is a skin over the custard, take it off; cut it into small cubes; add them to the boiling consommée and serve. This custard is called royal paste, or pâte royale.

PLAIN FAMILY SOUP.—Put two pounds of meat, with any bones or trimming you have—remnants of cold meat or gravy helps to enrich it—in a pot with three quarts of cold water; let them come slowly to a boil, and then *simmer* (see page 65) for two hours, skimming occasionally; add to the soup three teasponfuls of salt, one-half one of pepper, a carrot, a turnip, an onion, two cloves, a stick of celery and two sprigs of parsley if you have them.

If the vegetables are to be served with the soup, they must be very neatly cut, quite small; if the soup is to be strained, simply cut in thin slices will do. Let this slowly simmer two hours more; then put in a teaspoonful of caramel (see recipe); remove the meat; boil fast for a minute or two, to send up the fat, and skim off every bit of fat. If you find this difficult after the thickest fat is off, lay pieces of common butchers' paper or other unprinted paper on the surface till it no longer comes off greasy.

I need not repeat recipes which are, after all, the same thing, or should be. The clear soup may be varied into "macaroni" soup, "clear asparagus," or any of the many soups taking their name from the substances served in them, by adding any one of them to the stock, always remembering that they should be cooked thoroughly first and then put into the boiling stock.

Do not, however, use cold vegetables for the purpose.

ENGLISH CLEAR MOCK TURTLE.—This soup, as made by the English, is much richer than what is usually known in this country by the name. I give the best English method. Though more expensive it is not more troublesome than the more ordinary way, and when accomplished is a dish to set "before a king," or that gastronomous potentate, the Lord Mayor himself.

Get a calf's head; order the butcher to split it; remove the tongue and brains whole; lay these in vinegar and water till you need them, and take out the lining membrane of the nasal passages whole. Soak the head in salt and water, carefully washing where the brains have been; when all slime and blood are removed, put the head in a large soup-pot, and add to it six quarts of clear stock (see recipe). Slowly *simmer* for two hours after it has reached the boiling-point. Next take out the calf's head; cut all the meat from the bones; cut the flesh or skin into neat pieces two inches square. Lay them on a dish; to keep the pieces flat, lay another dish on the top of them. Pour any liquor that may have run from it, back into the stock-pot with all the bones; simmer for an hour longer; then strain it, and if not bright, clear it.

Mock turtle is a highly-flavored soup, yet very little too much herb would spoil it; to avoid all danger do as follows:

Put into a small saucepan three teaspoonfuls of chopped parsley, one of sweet basil, two of marjoram, two of savory, and one of lemon-thyme, two bay-leaves —any one making mock turtle often, would do well to keep a bottle of these herbs in these proportions, the parsley, however, always to be fresh, if possible. Pour half a pint of water on these; cover tightly and simmer for twenty minutes; take from the fire, and when cool, strain, pressing with a spoon to get as much of the flavor as you can. Next put your cleared soup back into the pot; put in the meat, or as much of it as you wish to serve, keeping the remains for an *entrée* (see recipe, Calf's Head with Hollandaise Sauce). The pieces of meat from the first cooking will probably be tender; if not, simmer them till they are. Now, add the juice of the herbs *gradually* till you have the flavor you desire; it may take the whole; next add a pint of pale sherry and the juice of a lemon, with salt and cayenne to taste.

If the soup is not a good color, add a teaspoonful or more of caramel.

Serve with egg-balls.

For half this quantity *everything* must be divided, but it keeps well in cool weather, being a very solid jelly when cold.

THICK MOCK TURTLE.—To make *Thick Mock Turtle*, proceed exactly as before ; only instead of using *clear stock*, any stock made from bones and scraps will do ; it will, of course, need no clearing ; thicken with brown thickening (see recipe), about one tablespoonful or more for each quart, and all the flavoring, egg-balls, etc., as in the last recipe.

MOCK TURTLE SOUP.—A fine American recipe.—Prepare a calf's head as already directed, saving tongue and brains. Lay in the bottom of the pot a carrot, a turnip, a small head of celery, three small onions, two large sprigs of parsley, two of thyme, one bay-leaf, one ounce of salt, and four cloves, and unless the flavor is objected to, half a pound of lean ham. On these lay the head ; then add seven quarts of water. Let it simmer three hours.

EGG BALLS FOR SOUPS.—Boil three eggs hard ; pound the yolks, adding a small teaspoonful of very finely chopped parsley, half a saltspoonful of fine salt, a quarter one of *while* pepper; moisten with raw yolk, and roll each ball in white of egg beaten only a little ; when well coated, dip into flour and drop into boiling water for two minutes.

MULLIGATAWNY SOUP.—This rich soup is best made with the excellent but despised rabbit. A fowl, however, can be substituted.

Take a small knuckle of veal, say three pounds, and one rabbit or fowl; if rabbit, lay it in water after cleaning.

Cut up the veal ; put the meat in a pot with two ounces of butter, a small slice of lean ham if approved, three onions and six apples peeled and cut up, and half a pint of cold water; set the stewpan on a hot fire, shaking it about occasionally till the bottom is covered with a brownish glaze; then add a carrot cut up, a turnip, three tablespoonfuls of curry powder, one of salt, and four tablespoonfuls of flour; mix all well together, and pour on a gallon of hot, not boiling, water; lay in the bones of the veal, and the chicken or rabbit cut up; let all simmer three hours. Take out the chicken or rabbit; trim some nice pieces to serve in the soup; keep the rest with a cup of the soup for an entrée (see recipe). Skim off all scum and fat as it rises; then strain the soup. Have some plain boiled rice to serve separate. The pieces of rabbit or chicken are either put in the soup or handed round with the rice.

Of course, the amount of curry powder may be reduced one-half if too hot.

FISH SOUPS.

FRENCH FISHERMAN'S SOUP.—Put a quarter pound of butter in a stewpan; when melted, add six ounces of flour; stir well together over a slow fire a few minutes; when cool, add a quart of milk and two quarts of stock; stir over the fire till boiling; cut the flesh from two flounders (or other firm fish); throw in the bones and trimmings to the soup, with four cloves, two bay-leaves, one spoonful of essence of anchovies, one of Harvey or Worcestershire sauce, half a saltspoonful of cayenne, a teaspoonful of sugar, one of salt (*three* if stock was unsalted); let the whole boil quickly for ten minutes, skimming well; cut the fish into neat pieces; lay it in a stewpan with a tablespoonful of finely chopped parsley; strain the soup through a fine strainer on to the fish;

let it cook ten minutes; add a gill of cream if you have it, and serve.

In place of stock, oyster liquor may be used.

BISQUE OF OYSTERS.—Put the liquor from one quart of oysters into a quart measure, filling it up with water; strain this into a large saucepan; lay aside half of the oysters, chop up the rest quite small, and put them to the liquor; let them stew fifteen minutes; have a quart of milk near boiling. Melt two ounces of butter in a saucepan; put two ounces of flour to it; stir till they bubble; then quickly pour the milk on to it, stirring all the time. When smooth, lay in the whole oysters; strain the oyster liquor to this, pressing the chopped oysters well, and season; let the whole just simmer three minutes after the oysters are put in, if they cook longer, they will become tough. Take it from the fire while you beat the yolks of two eggs one minute; then stir them into the bisque; stir for half a minute, but do not return the soup to the fire; serve in a hot tureen. Cut lemons should be handed round with bisques.

BISQUE OF CLAMS is made exactly in the same way as that of oysters, except that the clams should *all* be chopped fine and strained out, unless they are very tender.

BISQUE OF LOBSTER.—Take the meat from a fine boiled lobster, taking care to discard the spongy part, called "ladies' fingers"; also the sand-bag from the head and the entrail that runs through the body; carefully save the coral; wash the shell and claws carefully; bruise them, and put them to boil with one quart of water; put in also all but the coral and the firm white meat of the tail; cut this into small squares; bruise half the coral; stir it into the soup you are making, to color it a fine red. Take the rest, bruise it, mix it with fine cracker-dust, and moisten with *white* of egg till it forms a scarlet paste; make this into little balls. When the soup has cooked a quarter of an hour, put one ounce of butter in a stewpan, one ounce of flour, stir over the fire till they bubble; pour to it a quart of hot milk, stirring quickly; then strain to this the lobster liquor; stir and boil together till smooth; then drop in the pieces of flesh and the red balls (or if you wish to have lobster cutlets the same day or salad, the flesh need not be used; the soup is excellent without it); let them simmer one minute and serve.

WHITE SOUPS.

STOCK FOR WHITE SOUP.—Four pounds of knuckle of veal, one carrot, one turnip, two onions—all these of a fair size, about five ounces in weight of each vegetable—one bay-leaf, one clove, one saltspoonful of white pepper, one tablespoonful of salt, five quarts of water; let the veal with five quarts of water slowly simmer for two hours; then add the vegetables cut up; skim as the scum rises; cook another two hours and strain for use.

WHITE MUSHROOM SOUP.—One quart of stock, one quart of milk, one gill of thick cream, half a can of mushrooms and the liquor, two ounces of butter, two ounces of flour, one teaspoon of salt. Put both stock and milk to boil separately; stir in a saucepan over the fire the butter and flour together till they bubble; pour on half the milk quickly stirring all the time; add the rest, and then the stock; when thick as cream and smooth, put in the liquor of the mushrooms, the salt, the mushrooms, and last the cream. Just before serving squeeze in a teaspoonful of lemon-juice, or serve cut lemon with it.

If you have successfully made white sauce (see recipe), there will be no danger of any of these soups being lumpy; but if such a thing does occur, strain it before adding the mushrooms or other article.

WHITE ASPARAGUS SOUP.—Cut the points from a bundle of asparagus; lay them aside; cut up the rest of the rods quite small; if very hard you may bruise them; put them into a quart and half-pint of stock, and boil slowly till tender enough to go through a colendar; when all has been strained, put the points into the soup and let them boil till just tender—about ten minutes. Meanwhile put two ounces of butter and two ounces of flour into a saucepan on the fire; stir till they bubble; pour a quart of hot milk to this, a pint at a time, stirring all the time; then add the soup to it, the salt, and lastly one gill of cream. Serve.

CREAM SOUPS.—Under this name inexpensive easy soups are made without stock; they are very good, but of course lack the flavor of soups made with stock.

CREAM OF CAULIFLOWER.—Boil the white part of a small cauliflower twenty minutes in salted water. Put one quart of milk to boil; melt in a saucepan one ounce of butter and one ounce flour till they bubble, stirring thoroughly; pour in half the milk quickly, stirring till smooth; add the other half and boil a minute; then rub the cauliflower through a colander, stir it into the soup; season with a teaspoonful of salt and a quarter one of white pepper, and serve. The pulp of beets makes this "Cream of Beets," or of spinach "Cream of Spinach"; and the asparagus soup may be made in the same way if no stock is at hand. The stock, however, is such an improvement that I think most people, where economy is not a necessity, would prefer to use it.

GREEN PEA SOUP.—Shell half a peck of young peas; throw them into water. Put all the shells to boil in two quarts of any kind of stock, with four sprigs of parsley, six young onions, twelve mint leaves, and a handful of spinach (for color).

Let them boil one hour; rub them through a coarse wire sieve. The shells are troublesome, but a great deal can be got through with patience; pour back soup and pulp into a saucepan, let it boil; throw in the peas and boil till tender; season, and stir in a dessert-spoonful of white thickening, if not thick enough already. A beautiful color can be given by bruising a handful of spinach and squeezing it through a piece of cheese-cloth into the soup.

ICED CLARET SOUP FOR HOT WEATHER.—This is a Danish soup, but very welcome in summer in this climate.

Boil two ounces of sago in a pint of water until it is like thick mucilage; add to it a bottle of claret (with a little grated nutmeg, and two teaspoonfuls of sugar or not, as may be preferred); stir it well, strain it, and set it where it will be ice cold. Then serve as other soup.

Corn-starch may be used in place of sago, using two teaspoonfuls to thicken half a pint of water; let it boil ten minutes before adding the wine; then pour in the wine, stir, and strain, and season or leave unseasoned as may be preferred.

CHAPTER XXIV.

FISH.

SALMON WITH GREEN DUTCH SAUCE.—Take a piece of salmon two inches in thickness, if for a small family; put it on a plate, tie it in a napkin and put both in a saucepan of boiling water in which is plenty of salt—four teaspoonfuls to each quart, and a tablespoonful of vinegar—boil twenty minutes; serve on a napkin; garnish with parsley and lemon, or slices of cucumber, with green Dutch sauce (see recipe) in a sauce-boat.

BROILED SALMON, CAPER SAUCE.—The steaks should be an inch thick; dip each piece in flour, put it on a hot greased gridiron, turn it often for fifteen minutes, when it should be of a fine pale brown. Serve caper sauce (see recipe) in a boat.

CRIMPED COD MASKED WITH OYSTER SAUCE.

Take two or three pounds of codfish—crimped, if possible—lay on a plate set on a napkin; tie up the four corners, and put it into as much *boiling* water as will cover it, with one level tablespoonful of salt and the same of vinegar to the quart of water.

Scald two dozen oysters in their own liquor; let them get firm, but they must not boil; put a strainer on a bowl; pour them into it. Take the frill or beard from the oysters; put them back in the liquor. Put in a saucepan one good tablespoonful of butter, the same of flour; stir over the fire till they bubble; do not let them burn; pour the oysters and half a pint of the liquor to the butter and flour; stir till smooth and just boiling, then add one gill of cream; let it come again to the boiling point; season with white pepper, and very little salt, if the oyster liquor is not salt enough; pour this over the fish.

Thi sauce should be quite thick, so that it will not run off the fish but mask it. If the tablespoonful of flour was a quite full one it will be so, but if you have any doubts, don't put quite all the half-pint of oyster liquor until the cream is in; you can always make thinner, but without spoiling the oysters you cannot boil it down to get thick, as you would do for ordinary white sauce that is too thin.

Garnish with parsley and lemon.

HALIBUT WITH CAPER SAUCE.

Take a fine thick piece of halibut, unless you have a fish-boiler and strainer, put it on a plate, tie it in a napkin, place it in boiling water with a level tablespoonful of vinegar and one of salt to each quart. It will take twenty minutes after it has boiled. All fish should boil slowly to prevent breaking. When done take it up, pour over it a pint of thick caper sauce (see recipe); put round it a border of small new potatoes and tiny sprigs of parsley between them.

FILET DE SOLE EN BÉCHAMEL.

Bone two flounders (see Filet de Sole, page 57); put the bones and trimmings into a pint of water, with a half slice of onion and sprig of parsley; let them stew down to half pint, strain, and put aside. Roll up the eight filets after skinning them (see directions); tie them round, not too tightly, and trim them so that they will stand; put them in boiling milk, or water, with a teaspoonful of salt; boil slowly; when no longer transparent they are done; they take from seven to ten minutes according to size.

While they are cooking put a tablespoonful of butter in a saucepan with a tablespoonful of flour, stir till they bubble; pour the half pint of fish stock on it, stirring all the while. If you have cream, put half a gill less of stock and use cream in its place. This is now *béchamel*. Stand each little filet or turban (as a filet rolled is called) on a pretty dish; pour the sauce over them so that they are well coated; then ornament as follows:

Chop half a saltspoonful of parsley fine, and sprinkle over fish and sauce as evenly as possible; if the sauce is nice and thick, the parsley will rest on it. Have ready thin slices of green pickled gherkins, some bits of red pepper or capsicum skin, and if you can, the outer skin of pickled walnuts; each of these must be the size and thickness of a silver half dime. Place a piece on the top of each turban, alternately red, green, and black. If you have no walnut, use only the green and red. In garnishing this, or any other dish, always have everything ready before cooking, so that it may be quickly ornamented without getting cold.

FILET DE SOLE—FRIED.

See minute directions for the preparation of this dish in the first part of this book, page 57.

BAKED BLUEFISH.

This fish should be used very fresh. Choose one of fair size; wash it clean, taking care no slime or dark matter adheres to the inside. To remove it use your forefinger and some salt; wipe it dry, and stuff it with veal stuffing (see recipe), and sew it up; lay it in a dripping-pan with two ounces of butter in small pieces over it; sprinkle with a teaspoonful of salt; dredge it with flour, and bake in a good oven from half an hour to forty minutes, according to size. While it is cooking chop a tablespoonful of pickled cucumber, or half the quantity of capers, and a teaspoonful of parsley.

Take up the fish, put it to keep hot, set the dripping-pan on the stove; shake in it a dessert-spoonful of flour, and let it brown (or use brown flour, see recipe, which saves time); with the back of the spoon rub the flour into the butter and gravy that is in the pan; when brown and smooth, but not at all burnt, pour in quickly a cup of boiling water, and if you have it, a glass of claret wine, and pepper to taste; stir till all is smooth. Strain this sauce, put in a dessert-spoonful of Worcestershire sauce, one of anchovy sauce, and the chopped pickles and parsley. Serve the sauce in a separate vessel. Garnish the fish with lemon points and parsley, and serve.

STEWED CARP.

Cleanse carefully; lay the fish in a stew-pan with just enough broth of any kind to cover it and a teaspoonful of sweet herbs; stew very gently; when done take up the fish and strain the liquor; season with pepper and salt, a glass of claret, and a dessert-spoonful of Harvey sauce; thicken with a dessert-spoonful of brown thickening (see recipe), or one of flour and a teaspoonful of chopped parsley—skim off any fat—pour this over the fish and serve with small sippets of fried bread. A few small mushrooms are a great improvement.

STEWED CARP (FRENCH MODE).

Prepare as in last recipe. Lay the fish in a stewpan with a teaspoonful of salt; pour over it half a bottle of claret, with a slice of onion and a small piece of carrot cut fine, and a bouquet of herbs; stew gently till the fish is cooked; take up the fish, strain the wine, and thicken with a teaspoonful of corn-starch mixed in water; put in a little pepper, boil one minute, and pour over the fish.

FRIED SMELTS.

Choose them of an even size; wash them, wipe them dry, dip them in milk, then in flour. Beat up an egg with a tablespoonful of cold water; dip each fish, after shaking off superfluous flour, in the egg and then in sifted bread-crumbs, or cracker-dust; lay each one as you do it on a bed of cracker-dust. Have the lard in a deep kettle, just as if for doughnuts; when it is *very hot* and *smokes*, drop in a piece of bread; if it becomes pale brown in a few seconds, it is hot enough, if not, wait; drop in a piece more; if now hot enough, put in the fish, using a frying-basket if you have one; do not fry too many at a time. They should, if your fat was hot enough, be a beautiful yellow brown in *one minute*, if they are not, let it get hotter before you put the next lot in. Every one should be exactly the same pale color, and there will be no difficulty in this if the frying is done according to rule.

Serve with Tartar sauce or caper sauce (see recipe).

FISH, AU GRATIN.

This is a French mode of cooking fish very nice, and to those who use mushrooms frequently, not expensive, as they may probably have to open a can for another purpose.

Chop up one or two good-sized mushrooms, or half a can of them; a small piece of onion the size of a hickory nut; a teaspoonful of chopped parsley; a piece of lemon peel the size of a dime; a saltspoonful of salt, half one of pepper; put two ounces of butter in a saucepan, put in it the chopped onion, let it fry till tender; stir in one tablespoonful of flour, and, when smooth, half a pint of stock made from the bones, or any other you have, with a glass of white wine; when thick and smooth add the chopped mushrooms and parsley. Skin the fish, remove the bone, and cut it up in neat pieces. If you have no regular *gratin* dishes use any you can send to table. Butter it thickly, lay in the fish, pour the sauce over it, then cover thickly with dried bread-crumbs, shake over it some grated cheese, and bake. Have half a cup of butter melted, and when the *gratin* begins to brown, baste it all over with the butter, taking care there are no dry spots. This can, of course, be made without mushrooms, and lemon juice used instead of wine.

This one recipe will serve for any fish *au gratin*, and if the fish is boned early, the bones and trimmings will make the stock for the sauce.

BAKED BLACK FISH—AN EPICURE'S DISH.

Take a black fish of five pounds, cleanse and dry it thoroughly, flour it slightly, score the sides; put some sweet lard or beef dripping in a pan, and brown the fish on the top of the stove; pour off the lard and mix together the following ingredients: one teaspoonful of ground cloves, two-third teaspoonful of mace, one tablespoonful of salt, half saltspoonful of red pepper, two of black pepper, a large double handful of chopped onion, a large single handful of chopped parsley. Fill the scores in the sides of the fish with this seasoning, put the rest over the top; put sixteen balls of butter the size of a large walnut, each rolled in flour, upon the fish; pour into the pan a quarter pint of water for gravy.

(If more convenient, the fish may be prepared thus far early in the day and put aside until an hour before it is wanted.)

Put it in a good, moderate oven; it will take one hour to cook; fifteen minutes before it is done put in a dozen fine oysters and one pint of red wine. The oysters may be omitted if desirable.

Take up the fish very carefully, to avoid breaking; stir the gravy well round the pan to take off any of the clinging glaze; strain it and pour it round, *not over*, the fish; garnish with lemon points and little bunches of parsley.

CHAPTER XXV.

ENTRÉES.

Any small, dainty dish is proper for an entrée, from minced veal or beef, which is only glorified hash (see chapter on *warming over*), to salmon or game cutlets.

As a rule, I think an *entrée* should differ as far as possible from every other part of the dinner. For example, the day on which I had mock-turtle soup I would not have the entrée of calf's head; nor with oyster soup would I have oyster patties. Yet there are cases where circumstances, rather than taste, must be the guide.

The entrées are generally the weak point of a dinner, and are consequently the test of a good cook.

CALF'S HEAD, HOLLANDAISE SAUCE.

If you have made mock-turtle soup, you may have some of the meat remaining; simmer the pieces in enough of the soup, or some stock, to make them hot through; lay them in a dish (see recipe) and cover with half a pint of Hollandaise sauce; garnish with cut tomatoes—or tomato sauce may be used.

CALF'S HEAD, EN TORTUE.

Take any pieces that may be reserved from making soup, and a cup of the soup; melt one ounce of butter in a saucepan, stir in a tablespoonful of flour, pour in the cup of soup, stirring till smooth; strain into this the juice of a large ripe tomato, and the liquor from half a can of mushrooms and a dozen of the mushrooms; lay the pieces of meat in this sauce; let them stew for twenty minutes, taking great care they do not burn. Take them up and pour the sauce over them; have ready a saucepan or frying-kettle of *very hot* fat (see recipe); break into cups as many eggs as you have guests; drop them one by one into the smoking fat, just as if it were water and you were going to poach them; one minute ought to brown them, and fried in this way they will be quite *round*—do only one at a time, or while you take one out the other would harden—lay these round the dish; garnish with stoned olives or tiny gherkins.

CALF'S TONGUE STEWED.

Cut little fillets of salt pork; sprinkle them with a mixture of parsley, very finely-chopped chives (or onion), salt, and pepper; trim the tongue; parboil it to take off the skin; then lard it with these fillets (see Larding); put in a small stone crock with a lid, two slices of fat pork, two sprigs of parsley, two of thyme, one bay leaf, one clove, half an onion, one carrot cut in slices, a saltspoonful of salt, and half one of pepper; lay the tongue on the vegetables, etc.; pour in half a glass of wine and a glass of broth or soup; cover it; set it in a moderate oven for three hours and a half, keeping it well covered.

Take up the tongue, lay it in a dish, strain the gravy to it, and either surround it with green peas, string beans, or tomato sauce.

CALF'S BRAINS, AU BEURRE NOIR.

Soak the brains in one tablespoonful of vinegar and one quart of water; carefully remove all the fibrous skin that surrounds them without breaking them; put them in boiling water well salted, and with them a small bunch of parsley, a saltspoonful of powdered marjoram, and one of thyme; let them boil gently twenty minutes; while they are doing so, fry some rounds of bread the size of the top of a teacup and half an inch thick, in very hot fat. Take up the brains, drain them, divide them, and put a neat piece on each round of fried bread; stick a piece of red beetroot in the top of each piece of brain and pour over them the *beurre noir* (see recipe).

SWEETBREADS, FRIED.

When they come from the butcher they should be put immediately into salt and water to take out any dark blood; leave them an hour, then parboil them for ten minutes, drain them, and drop them into cold water; remove all loose thick skin and gristle, but do not break them; dry them, flour them, and then roll them in egg and bread-crumbs or cracker-dust; fry them a rich light brown. If large, they should be split before crumbing; serve round a mound of green peas, and béchamel or tomato sauce in a boat.

SWEETBREADS STEWED WITH MUSHROOMS.

Prepare a pair of sweetbreads by parboiling and skinning (see last recipe), then lard them all over the top; lay some slices of fat pork in a stewpan, also a teaspoonful of chopped onion, two of carrot, a stick of celery, and two sprigs of parsley; the vegetables must be finely minced; lay the sweetbreads on these; add a cup of stock, but not enough to cover the sweetbreads; let them *slowly* stew one hour; then take up the sweetbreads and set them with *the larded side up* in the oven till they are *pale brown;* strain the gravy, rubbing as much through the sieve as you can; put it back in a saucepan, thicken with a teaspoonful of roux; put in a dozen and a half of canned mushrooms; let it boil a minute; put the sweetbreads on a dish, pour the mushrooms in the centre and the gravy round. If the stock should have dried away, boiling water or more stock can be added.

SWEETBREADS, THE SIMPLEST WAY.

Parboil and skin them; cut them up in small pieces; put a tablespoonful of butter in a saucepan; when hot, drop the sweetbreads in with a saltspoonful of salt; let them cook slowly twenty minutes, occasionally shaking them; take them out; stir a teaspoonful of flour into the butter, and add half a cup of broth or water, stirring carefully; boil till thick and smooth; return the sweetbread; let it stew a minute, and serve either on squares of toast or with three-cornered pieces of toast sticking round it.

VEAL CUTLETS.

Take the cutlets from the middle of the leg; let them be cut an inch thick; divide into small shapely pieces; pound each piece with a rolling-pin till they are half an inch thick; squeeze a few drops of lemon juice over each and pile them up one on the other for a couple of hours or until you want to use them. The lemon juice makes them very tender. Season them with salt, and egg and bread-crumb them (see directions) carefully. Although it is customary to speak of *fried* veal cutlets, they are usually fried in just enough fat, for which process there seems no proper English term but "*dry frying.*" Veal cutlets are one of the few things better cooked in this way than immersed in boiling fat. The reason is, because they require to cook more slowly than most other things.

Put in a pan two large tablespoonfuls of beef dripping, if you have it, or lard, and any fat belonging to the cutlets; let it get thoroughly hot; lay in the cutlets and let them get pale brown one side before you turn them; do this with a cake turner, carefully—they will take from twelve to fifteen minutes, for they require to be thoroughly done. Take them up and pour the fat out of the pan, put in it a dessert-spoonful of brown thickening, and when it has melted pour in a cup of cream and hot water, or broth; stir well, rubbing all the gravy from the pan; put in a saltspoonful of salt, quarter of pepper. Dress the cutlets on a dish and pour the gravy round, not over them.

For those who like ham, they may be served with a small slice of ham to each cutlet, and the ham being fried first, the cutlets are fried in the fat from it, instead of lard.

MUTTON OR LAMB CHOPS BREADED.

These must be nicely trimmed, only about the third of an inch of fat left on the outside; and, if they are loin chops, the soft flap end turned round, horseshoe fashion; if rib chops, cut an inch and a half of the meat from the bone and scrape it.

Egg and crumb them (see directions), and drop them

into very hot fat. Mutton chops will take one minute to cook, lamb chops two minutes. If the fat has been properly hot, the former will be a rich brown outside and pink within, in that time. The lamb chops require to be well done.

The chops may be laid round a mound of green peas, string beans, or mashed potatoes.

CHICKEN CROQUETTES.

Take the flesh of half a chicken, or rather more than half a box of boned chicken (I find for croquettes the boned chicken quite as good, and a great saving of work); chop the chicken, and with it half a can of mushrooms, or half a dozen large oysters.

Put a good tablespoonful of butter in a saucepan with a tablespoonful of flour; stir over the fire till they bubble; put into a half-pint measure a gill of strong stock, half a gill of cream, and liquor of oysters or mushrooms to make two gills; pour this on to the butter and flour, stir till a *thick* sauce is formed; then put in the chopped chicken and mushroom, with half a saltspoonful of pepper, one of salt, and a teaspoonful of lemon juice; stir well, taking care that it does not burn. Take it off the fire—it should be a sort of thick mush, and very creamy; butter two plates; turn it out and spread the mixture on them; put it on the ice so that it may get cold and firm.

When quite firm cut the mixture into strips, form it between the hands into rolls like corks, or small pears; if the latter, have ready some short willow or other twigs to insert after they are crumbed. Be very careful not to have the croquettes too large or they will burst in frying. The quantity given will make from twelve to fifteen.

Have at least a pound of cracker-powder on a board; roll each one in it; have an egg beaten with a dessert-spoonful of water; dip each croquette in the egg and again in the cracker-dust, laying them as you do them on a dish well strewed with cracker-powder. In crumbing use one hand to pass the croquettes through the egg, the other to crumb them.

Have the fat exceedingly hot, so that the bread you try with colors in thirty seconds; arrange the croquettes in a frying-basket not more than six at a time, and immerse them; the fat must be deep enough to cover the croquettes, and they should brown in *two minutes;* they are then done. Lift the frying-basket out, stand it on brown paper, and lift each croquette out carefully on to a hot dish; lay in half a dozen more and fry them. Croquettes look better garnished with fried parsley than anything else.

CHICKEN RISSOLES.

Make the same mixture as for croquettes; indeed, in cold weather and when only a small dish of croquettes is required, a part of the mixture can be kept for two or three days, by covering it with buttered paper, and then used for rissoles or fritters. If you have no pastry ready, rub three ounces of butter into four ounces of flour; wet with cold water to make a stiff, smooth paste. Flour a pastry-board and rolling-pin, and roll the paste out as *thin* as possible; cut it in pieces four inches long and three wide. Roll the chicken mixture into small sausage-like forms, the thickness of your finger; lay them on the paste, wet the edges and roll it over the chicken, pressing the paste together smoothly that they may not burst. Egg and crumb these just the same as croquettes and fry in the same way, only rissoles require four minutes to cook instead of two. Serve them log-house fashion with fried parsley in the middle.

CHICKEN FRITTERS.

This is again the same mixture as for croquettes and rissoles, but the fritter is a delicious variety. Make some *thick* frying-batter (see recipe); make the chicken mixture into balls the size of a walnut; flatten them a little. Have the fat very hot, the batter ready, and then drop each ball into the batter, which must be made thick enough to coat them so that the meat is not seen through it; instead of arranging these in the frying-basket as you would croquettes, have the basket in the fat and drop each fritter from the end of a spoon into it. The fat must be hot enough to make the batter puff up at once; when a rich brown they are done. Lift out the basket, drain, and serve with fried parsley.

KROMESQUIES OF CHICKEN

Are the same as rissoles, only instead of the minced chicken being enveloped in paste, very thin slices of fat pork are used, fastened with wooden toothpicks, and they are then crumbed and fried. They are more difficult than croquettes or rissoles, but very delicious. They may be served in a rich brown sauce (see recipe).

VARIATIONS ON THE FOUR FOREGOING RECIPES.

Turkey, veal, or beef may be used for any of these four dishes, instead of the chicken. A little onion or ham, or any flavoring preferred, may be substituted for the mushrooms or oysters, although nothing is so good as these.

CHICKEN FRICASSEE.

Prepare a chicken as directed (see preparation of poultry). Cut each leg and wing in two at the joint; cut the back in two; the stomach makes one piece. With the gizzard and neck there should be thirteen pieces.

Throw the pieces into boiling water for one or two minutes, take out and drain them. Put in a stewpan a tablespoonful of butter, one of flour; when they bubble add half a pint of water or broth, two sprigs of parsley, a pinch of grated nutmeg, four small onions, a small teaspoonful of salt, a saltspoonful of white pepper, then the chicken. Cover closely, and when it reaches the boiling point draw aside where it will simmer slowly and not burn. Shake it round every few minutes. If slowly cooked and closely covered, the sauce will not dry away much; if it should do so, add a little more broth or boiling water. When it has cooked one hour, if young, it will be done; if an old fowl it will take two. Take up the meat and keep it hot, strain the sauce, unless the onion is liked in it. Put it back in the stewpan with a dozen small mushrooms and a little of their liquor, let it boil one minute, then beat the yolks of two eggs with a tablespoonful of milk. Take the saucepan to a cool place, wait one minute, then stir in the beaten yolks. Put the saucepan back on the stove, stir till it is a thick, smooth, yellow cream, but it *must not boil* or the eggs will curdle and the appearance be spoilt.

Arrange the chicken on the dish in the following way: The neck, gizzard, forepart of the back, and drumsticks in the middle, one upper part of leg on each side the dish, one wing beside each, then the breast and hind part of the back, the ends of the wings top and bottom. Squeeze a few drops of lemon juice into the sauce, lay the mushrooms over the meat and pour the sauce over all. Serve.

This is decidedly the best way to make the dish, but more difficult than the following, because it requires watching or it will burn.

SIMPLER MODE FOR FRICASSEE.

Prepare the chicken as before, put it in a stewpan with half a pint of water, one large or four small onions, two sprigs of parsley, a pinch of nutmeg, a scant teaspoonful of salt, a saltspoonful of pepper; lay in the chicken; cook as before. When done, take it out, put a tablespoonful of butter and a small one of flour into a small saucepan; cook till they bubble, strain the gravy from the chicken, to this, stir till smooth, add the yolks of two eggs, beaten with a tablespoonful of milk; when it has cooled one minute stir in a hot spot but do not boil; pour this sauce over the chicken, arranged as in last recipe. The mushrooms may be added or not, as convenient.

Little squares or crescents of rough puff paste, baked and laid round either of these fricassees are a very nice addition and serve to garnish.

FRICASSEE OF VEAL

Is made in the same way, but is improved by forcemeat balls, poached (see recipe), and laid round.

SALMI OF DUCK OR GAME.

Strictly speaking, a salmi differs from warmed-over duck or game, because the birds are only supposed to be half cooked on purpose for it.

Entrées.

But, as a matter of fact, an excellent salmi can be prepared from birds that have already done duty for dinner, provided they were not overcooked and the sauce made very rich.

Cut up the cold bird into neat joints, take away all skin and gristle, take all bones that are bare of meat, bruise them well; lay the meat in a saucepan and put it aside; lay the bones, skin and trimmings with any gravy in another saucepan, into which put a small carrot, an onion, a teaspoonful of salt, quarter one of pepper, two sprigs of parsley, a clove, a blade of mace, a bay leaf, a saltspoonful of thyme, an ounce of butter. The carrot and onion must be cut very fine. Let all these fry in the butter till they are all colored light brown, then put in half a pint of broth or water and a gill of wine, red or white, with one lump of sugar. Let all stew, well covered, till reduced to one-half; then make half a pint of brown sauce (see recipe), if you have none ready; put it to the bones and vegetables, let them stew another half hour. Then strain, taste if seasoned enough, and pour into the saucepan with the meat. Leave them a quarter of an hour to come back to boiling point, but *not to boil*. Dish the bird, let the sauce boil fast to reduce it, skimming it well. When there is only enough to serve with the meat pour it over it; serve with fried sippets round the dish, on each of which may be a stoned olive, or half a spoonful of red currant jelly if approved.

SALMI SAUCE.

The sauce made as above is called by professional cooks "Salmi Sauce"; it is not troublesome to make, and is equally good for warming over slices of cold beef or mutton.

SALMON CROQUETTES.

Take the remains of dressed salmon, free from the skin and bone, which should be bruised and boiled for stock in a pint of water until reduced to *half a pint;* tear the flesh into shreds; make a béchamel sauce of the fish stock, using a full tablespoonful of butter, the same of flour (see recipe); when thick and smooth add a gill of thick cream, a glass of sherry or white wine, and the beaten yolks of two eggs—these must be stirred in last and allowed to come to the boiling point but *not to boil;* then put in half a pound of salmon flakes. It should be as thick as oatmeal porridge; when turned on to a buttered plate it should spread, *but not run;* spread it an inch thick on a plate and set on ice to get quite cold. When wanted for use divide into pieces, shape into the form of corks, egg and crumb them (see Crumbing) and fry two minutes in very hot fat.

Dipped into frying batter these are excellent. Garnish with fried parsley, and serve with cucumber salad.

LOBSTER CUTLETS AND CROQUETTES.

Take the meat from a good-sized lobster; put a tablespoonful of butter and one of flour in a saucepan on the fire; stir till they bubble; pour into it a gill of water, a gill of cream, and a glass of white wine; stir till thick and smooth; beat the yolks of two eggs; stir them in with the meat of the lobster, and enough of the coral bruised to make the whole a fine red; stir it over the fire till it is at boiling point; turn the mixture out on a buttered plate and set it to harden. Flour your hands and form the mixture when cold into cutlets, as near as you can, the shape and size of a small lamb cutlet. Crumb them as directed for croquettes;

stick one of the small lobster claws in the end of each cutlet to represent the bone. Arrange in the frying-basket very carefully and fry in very hot fat.

Lobster croquettes are made from the same mixture, but formed into cork or cone shapes.

ROUGH PUFF PASTE.

(South Kensington School of Cookery.)

This pastry will serve for most purposes for which puff paste is used; it is better than most home-made puff paste, and takes no longer to make than common short paste, while puff paste is the most laborious work of the kitchen.

Have the butter as hard as possible, the chopping-bowl and knife cold. Take eight ounces of flour and six of butter; put them in a chopping-bowl and chop together, not too fine; make a hole in the centre of the flour and butter, in which put the yolk of one egg, a quarter saltspoonful of salt and a teaspoonful of lemon juice and a tablespoonful of ice-water; break the egg in this water with a knife; then slowly and lightly mix it all with the fingers, using more water if necessary to form a *stiff* paste. Handle it lightly; keep the hands and board well floured that the paste may not stick.

Take the rolling-pin, flour it, and roll out the paste into an oblong sheet half an inch thick; fold it one-third over, then the other third over that (you have now a neat piece of three thicknesses); turn the rough edges toward you, roll it out again, and fold in the same way; do so once more, always turning the rough edges toward you, and it is ready to use at once; but if the day is hot and you have time to lay it on the ice for a short time it will be better; also, if during the process of rolling it shows signs of sticking, laying it *on* the ice in a tin for a few minutes, will make your work the easier.

The only art in this pastry is to follow directions *exactly*, and to handle lightly. Many will say, "I have not a light hand." I answer: Every woman has a light hand if she is handling white satin or velvet. Handle pastry as delicately as if it were satin or velvet and the pile would crush.

Before using this paste, read chapter on Pastry (part first); all that relates to using puff paste applies to this.

This paste made one day, or only mixed, and once rolled and folded, and finished and used the next, is always better, and in ice may be kept two or three days and be the better for it.

I find it a good plan in summer when I want to make paste, to put chopping-bowl and knife and rolling-pin in or on the ice-box, and have the pastry board as cool as you can. With soft butter and warm tools you can never have flaky or light paste.

Patties are among the most acceptable entrées, and with the South Kensington rough puff paste very easy to make, although the cases can be bought ready at a pastry cook's and filled at home.

PATTY CASES.

Take some rough puff paste; roll it a third of an inch thick, not less; have a medium-sized biscuit cutter and one quite small, about the size of a silver dollar; cut out three times as many rounds with the large cutter as you want patties—eighteen if you want six; pile them three together, wetting the two under ones slightly to make them adhere. You have now six patties rather over an inch thick; take the small cutter, dip it in flour, shake off any that may cling, and press it on each patty, cutting only *half way* through. Take the patties up on a cake turner, and slip them on to a baking tin; brush each one over with yolk of egg beaten with a tablespoonful of water; set them in a hot oven to bake. If you have had your paste cold, and handled it lightly and quickly, these will rise to three inches in height. They require fifteen minutes to bake. When they are pale brown all over, take them out; let them stand one minute; then take off the small piece in the centre—it will have risen perhaps out of its place—if not, with a sharp-pointed knife lift it out; then take a small spoon and dig out the soft paste inside, leaving only a crust about half an inch thick, but be very careful there are no holes in the walls or sides; replace the tops and they are ready to fill with either of the following three mixtures, or any other you may choose:

LOBSTER PATTIES.

Pick out the firm white flesh of a hen lobster; cut it into small dice. Put a large teaspoonful of flour and *two* of butter into a saucepan on the stove; let them bubble; pour to it a gill of cream or milk; stir till smooth; then add a teaspoonful of the pounded coral to make a bright pink sauce, and a teaspoonful of anchovy sauce, if you have it; take it from the fire when it has boiled two or three minutes; beat the yolk of an egg with a teaspoonful of cold milk, and stir it in gradually; keep on stirring, and add the lobster meat at the same time; set it on the fire again and let it come to the boiling point, *but not boil* or the egg will curdle. It should now look like chopped lobster in *very thick* red cream or custard.

If you need to keep it hot, do so in a saucepan of hot water; fill the patty cases neatly, put the top on and put them in the oven; but serve them before they get so hot that the inside cooks, or the egg will curdle and the pastry be spoiled.

N. B.—Always put the filling in patties *hot*, or it will not warm through till the patties are spoiled.

OYSTER PATTIES.

Take a dozen and a half Blue Points; scald them in their own liquor, being careful they do not remain in it a moment after it boils; take them out; cut each oyster into four pieces, if they are large; put a dessert-spoonful of butter in a small saucepan with a dessert-spoonful of flour; pour to this one gill of the liquor strained and one gill of cream or milk; a saltspoonful of salt and half one of white pepper; boil all, stirring till smooth; beat the yolks of two eggs, add this with the cut-up oysters to the sauce; let all get hot together, stirring all the time; it must be *very* thick, which it will be just before the boiling point; take it from the fire quickly, stirring all the time to prevent the eggs curdling; add a few drops of lemon juice and just a suspicion of nutmeg.

These and lobster patties *should* be served on a silver dish with fried parsley and a small crayfish in each corner of the dish, if obtainable.

CLAM PATTIES.

These are so very good that I think if they were better known they would meet with favor.

Take small clams; scald them in their own liquor; take out the hard part, and proceed exactly as for oysters.

SALMON PATTIES.

Prepare as lobster patties, using salmon instead of the lobster.

CHICKEN PATTIES.

Take the white meat of a chicken ; cut it (not chop it) into small dice ; take the chicken bones and trimmings, if you have no stock ready ; pound them well ; put them into a pint of water with an ounce of carrot cut fine, a sprig of parsley, a stick of celery, if you have it, and a small onion, and a saltspoonful of salt ; stew these slowly two hours; strain the stock or broth ; put the liquor from half a can of mushrooms or a gill of oyster liquor with it, and boil it as fast as possible till there is about a gill left; put a gill of cream and the chicken into this; thicken with a tablespoonful of flour, and one of butter cooked in a separate saucepan ; pour the chicken and liquor on to it, and stir till it all boils *gently;* take it off at once ; two or three chopped oysters or a dozen mushrooms improve it greatly ; fill the cases with the hot filling, and serve on a napkin or silver dish.

DRESDEN PATTIES.

These cases are no trouble at all to an expert in frying, and are elegant and economical.

Take *stale baker's* bread cut in thick slices ; with a biscuit cutter of medium size cut rounds two inches thick. Make a custard of two eggs and a pint of milk; season it with salt, of course no sugar; pour it into a dish and set the rounds of bread in it, taking care they are well covered; turn them gently from time to time so that they may get well soaked, but they must not break ; if there is any sign of them getting too soft to hold together take them out; usually an hour suffices to soak them; let them drain ten minutes; then you may either flour the outside or roll them in egg and cracker-dust. Have the frying-kettle with plenty of fat in it, which must be hot enough to color bread in half a minute; set the soaked pieces of bread in the frying-basket, using a cake-turner to take them up. They must be very gently handled. Set the frying-basket in the hot fat and fry till they are a fine light brown. Take them up and with a sharp-pointed knife cut a circle in the top, leaving a border of half an inch all round; with a spoon dig out a good deal of the soft custard-like centre; fill this either with the same preparation as for chicken or oyster patties, with sweetbreads, or with preserves, jelly, or marmalade. If they are filled with meat of any kind garnish with parsley.

A FEW OLD-FASHIONED PLAIN DISHES.

IRISH STEW.

Cut half a dozen lean chops from the neck of mutton; flour them and lay them in a saucepan or stewpan with two onions cut in slices, and a teaspoonful of butter; put them over a quick fire and let all brown lightly, stirring occasionally to prevent burning; when the onions are a light brown pour in a pint of cold water. Skim off the fat that will rise to the top; put in a good teaspoonful of salt, a level saltspoonful of white pepper, and set the saucepan where it will simmer *very gently;* when it has been simmering an hour and a half, skim it carefully; put in a teaspoonful of Worcestershire sauce, and taste if the gravy is well seasoned. Then

Entrées.

put in half a dozen large (or more if small) potatoes cut in half; cover *closely* and simmer another hour. The potatoes do not require to be covered with the gravy, they simply steam over the meat; sufficient good rich gravy for the meat is all that is necessary; to cover the potatoes with liquid, as is often done, is to make a quantity of *broth*, but no gravy.

Arrange the chops in the centre of a dish, the potatoes round, and pour the gravy over all.

HARICOT OF MUTTON (SIMPLE).

Take some nice rib chops; trim off all but very little fat; flour them, lay them in a stewpan and brown them well and quickly, taking care that they do not burn; cut up a carrot and a turnip into neat pieces, and a large onion; put them in with the chops, a teaspoonful of salt, quarter one of pepper, and water enough to cover them, no more; let them simmer very gently two hours and a half; skim carefully to remove all grease. Take up the chops; arrange them on a dish round a mound of neatly-cut string beans; arrange the carrot and turnip neatly round the chops and put them to keep hot, while you stir a dessert-spoonful of brown thickening if you have it (see recipe for Roux or Brown Thickening) into the gravy (or else use butter and brown flour). Let it boil; taste for seasoning, and strain it over the meat and vegetables.

STEWED BEEFSTEAK.

Take two pounds of round steak; cut in pieces the size to serve; flour them, and sprinkle with pepper and salt; lay them in a stewpan with two dessert-spoonfuls of vinegar, and cover closely; place the stewpan where it will gently cook, and leave it one hour. Then take off the cover; cut into it one onion, one small carrot, one small turnip, and pour in half a pint of hot water; cover again and let it simmer two hours longer. Take up the meat and keep it hot. Stir into the gravy, if you have them, a teaspoonful of Worcestershire and one of mushroom catsup, or Harvey sauce, with a teaspoonful of brown thickening; strain it, rubbing all the vegetables you can through the strainer; let it boil up and pour it over the meat. If preferred, the vegetables may be left in and served with the steak.

SEA PIE.

This old-fashioned English dish is very good in winter.

Take two pounds of meat; if you buy it on purpose, use part *lean* mutton and part beef, or beef, mutton, and veal; although mutton or beef alone will do; put them into a saucepan with just water to cover them; cut quite small, two onions, half a small carrot, and half a turnip, with two heaped saltspoons of salt, and a half one of pepper; put to the whole a pint and half of water; let the whole stew slowly two hours. Meanwhile make a suet crust (see recipe for Suet Crust) of six ounces of suet and ten of flour; roll it out till it will about fit the saucepan, and an inch thick or rather less. Skim the gravy, when it has cooked two hours, removing all fat; taste if salt enough, and add sauce for flavoring if you choose. Then put on the suet crust for cover, making it fit over the meat closely; for this reason take care that you rolled it large enough; if too large never mind, let it turn up at the sides a little. Put on the cover of the saucepan and cook slowly another hour. It must cook *slowly* or the meat will be stringy; it must not *stop* cooking or the crust will be heavy.

When done, cut the crust across pie-fashion; lift out each of the pieces and lay them round a dish, then pour meat and gravy in the centre and serve.

CHAPTER XXVI.

ROASTS.

ROAST BEEF.

Very full directions are given in Chapter VIII for roasting of all kinds. Yet to save referring back, I repeat the recipes, remarking that if you roast one thing well, and know *why* you do it, you can roast all.

A piece of ribs of beef weighing eight pounds will take an hour and quarter to an hour and half, according to whether you like it rare or well done.

Set the joint on a wire stand in a dripping-pan; dust it over with flour, but do not season it; put it in *a hot* oven; meat put in a cool oven, and both allowed to get hot together, will neither be sightly nor toothsome; baste it frequently.

If you choose, and your meat is fat enough to warrant it, you may put a few peeled potatoes in the dripping-pan, sprinkling them with salt, and turning them about when you baste the meat, so that they may brown; turn the joint over when it has been one hour in the oven, so that it may brown equally.

When the meat is done it should look of a rich dark mahogany color, brown all over but nowhere burnt. Take it up on a hot dish; if you have potatoes put them round it. Set the dripping-pan on the stove; having poured off the fat carefully, and pour into it a cup of boiling water; with a spoon remove every scrap of the sticky dark substance that clings to the pan, it will all dissolve on the back of the spoon; put in one saltspoon of salt and a little pepper; let this boil two or three minutes on the stove till dark and rich; then serve it in a sauce-boat; sprinkle the beef with fine salt, garnish it with parsley and horse-radish *scraped* (if you have patience and a sharp knife), it is far better than the ground horse-radish in flavor, and of course the long, delicate shreds are more ornamental, little tufts of the white and green alternately are a pretty garnish.

FILLET OF BEEF.

Trim it very carefully; remove the gristly skin from it, if the butcher has not done so; this must be carefully done not to disfigure the fillet; round off the ends and any superfluous fat; in short, make it a neat, compact piece of meat. Lard it, (see Larding).

Set it in a dripping-pan on a wire stand, with some beef *fat*, not *suet*, for basting. Half an hour to three-quarters, if very large, will cook it in a hot oven.

Serve with brown mushroom sauce.

ROAST LEG OF MUTTON.

Rub the skin of a leg of mutton with salt (from the skin there is no gravy to draw out); flour it lightly; set it in a dripping-pan without water, and put it in a hot oven; an hour and a half will cook a medium-sized leg, unless liked well done, when it will take a quarter of an hour more.

When done take it from the pan, set it on a hot dish, and put it to keep hot. Pour the dripping off very carefully from the corner of the pan, changing the corner when the dark sediment begins to run, as you wish to save that, yet get rid of all grease; set the pan on the stove and pour into it a small cup of water, with a saltspoonful of salt; rub off all the gravy and dark substance from the pan; let it boil till all is dissolved, then pour through a strainer into sauce-tureen and serve.

ROAST SADDLE OF MUTTON.

Have the saddle neatly trimmed and superfluous fat removed; skin it and skewer the skin over it till it is nearly done.

Set it in the oven one hour and a half before it is wanted, if it weighs about six pounds; the oven must of course be hot; baste frequently, and half an hour before it is done take off the skin; dredge the saddle with flour; sift a little fine salt over it, and put it in a part of the oven where it will brown well without burning.

Take it up on a very hot platter, pour the fat carefully from the dripping-pan, put in a cup of hot water, rub off all the glaze or gravy on the pan, season with salt and put into the gravy a glass of claret and a spoonful of red currant jelly; serve the gravy in a tureen.

The saddle should be carved lengthwise of the joint.

ROAST LAMB.

Lamb requires to be very thoroughly cooked. A leg of lamb is roasted exactly as a leg of mutton. One weighing four to five pounds will take an hour and half. Serve with mint sauce (see recipe).

ROAST FILLET OF VEAL.

No meat requires more careful cooking than roast veal. Any meat more insipid than plain unsavory veal is not to be imagined. The less condiment there is about roast beef or mutton the better, but veal requires a great deal.

The handsomest joint of veal is the fillet, as the part of the leg from which the cutlet is cut is called. Take a piece about five pounds; remove the bone in the centre, fill it with veal forcemeat (see recipe); also make a pocket with your finger between the skin and the flesh and lay forcemeat in it. Skewer the veal; bind it firmly into a round shape, and flour it; cover it with very thin slices of fat pork; set it on a wire stand in a dripping-pan and put it in a moderate oven. Veal requires very thorough cooking and will take half an hour to the pound. Therefore great care must be taken that it does not burn before it comes out of the oven; it should be often basted, and be a bright, dark brown all over. If pork is objected to, spread butter over it before putting it in the oven.

Just before it is taken out make half a pint of butter sauce (see recipe). Then place the meat on a platter; take away all the bits of pork, set the dripping-pan on the stove and pour the sauce into it, send it round with your spoon into every part till all the glaze or hardened gravy is dissolved and the whole a nice brown. Remove the strings and skewers from the meat and pour a little of the brown gravy round it; serve the rest in a tureen. Garnish with cut lemon.

ROAST FILLET OF VEAL WITH MUSHROOMS OR OYSTERS.

Prepare a fillet as in the last recipe, only do not remove the bone in the centre; roast in the same way. While it is cooking take a dozen large oysters, or more if small, scald them in their own liquor; take them up, strain the liquor, stir an equal quantity of cream and a tablespoonful of white thickening (see recipe for Blanc, page 34), a little salt and cayenne into it, and boil till thick. Take up the meat; with a very sharp knife cut out the bone, and a good piece of meat round it so as to leave a cavity. Set the meat on a platter, put it to keep quite hot. Quickly take all the veal (free from gristle) from the bone and chop it with the oysters; stir it into the sauce you have made; it should be about as stiff as mush. Make all hot together and pour it into the cavity of the veal. Make gravy as in the last recipe. Mushrooms chopped and stewed in butter may be used instead of the oysters if preferred.

ROAST VEAL AND MACARONI (AN ITALIAN DISH).

Prepare a fillet or shoulder of veal as directed, but without pork; set it in the oven. Boil some macaroni, broken into six-inch lengths, till tender. When the veal is within half an hour of being done, cleanse and trim some mushrooms; cut them up, sprinkle salt over them, and lay them in the dripping-pan with the macaroni. When you take up the meat lay the macaroni round the dish, the mushrooms over it; have drawn butter or béchamel sauce ready to pour into the pan; boil it up and strain it, taking care to rub all you can of the bits of mushroom and glaze through the strainer. Serve the gravy in a tureen.

ROAST SHOULDER OF VEAL, STUFFED.

Get the butcher to bone the shoulder; cut off the knuckle part and use it for stock with the bones (when you have meat boned take care to have the bones sent home); fill the cavity where the blade bone was with good forcemeat (see recipe for veal forcemeat); skewer it and flour it; cover with fat pork, butter, or nice beef dripping, and bake it, allowing half an hour for each pound; pour off the fat, if any, from the dripping-pan, and make gravy as directed for roast fillet of veal.

ROAST LOIN OF VEAL.

Make a pocket with your finger between the skin and flesh of the veal and insert the forcemeat, or slices of fat pork if preferred; skewer it securely, flour it, put buttered paper over the kidney, and rub the skin with a little salt and put it in the oven; remove the paper half an hour before serving. Make gravy as directed for roast fillet of veal.

ROAST LOIN OF PORK.

Select quite young pork with very small bones, the middle of the loin is the best part; if lean enough for the rind to be left on, score it thoroughly, for the sake of the carver, but not too deeply; the scores less than half an inch apart; a sharp, strong penknife is best for the purpose; rub the pork over with flour, salt, and sage leaves, dried on a plate, and rubbed to powder.

Set it in the dripping-pan and bake in a moderate oven, allowing half an hour to each pound. It must be well browned, but not burnt. When done take up the meat, pour the fat from the corner of the dripping-pan, taking care to keep back the sediment; pour hot water into the pan, set it on the stove, dissolve all the dried gravy with a spoon, and let it boil; skim off the fat which the boiling will send up, and season; serve the gravy in a tureen, with apple sauce in another.

CHAPTER XXVII.

POULTRY.

PREPARATION OF POULTRY.

Chickens, ducks, capons and turkeys should be killed at least twenty-four hours before cooking; the following directions as to cleansing and preparing apply to all kinds of poultry.

When well picked, singe by removing the stove cover and putting some paper in, pass the bird over the flame, taking care not to blacken it or burn the skin.

Cut the neck off as near the body as possible, pushing the skin down before you do it, so as to leave enough skin to cover the place where the neck has been cut; cut off the feet below the joint; with your forefinger loosen the crop, and take it out without breaking or emptying it. Next cut a slit right under the rump large enough to run two fingers, if a chicken or duck; your hand, if a turkey or goose, into the body. Before attempting to draw out the entrails, loosen with your finger all the tiny strings that attach them to the body, be sure that your fingers can pass between the contents of the stomach and the body in *every* direction without obtruction; then bend your hand or fingers round the mass and draw it forward, this will bring the whole out in a ball; by no means drag it by any particular part, or you will break the entrails or gall bladder, and the whole process, in the former case, be an unclean one; in the latter, the bird may be spoiled, for it is impossible to wash away the bitter of the gall if broken. Cut off the vent which will free the main entrail. If properly managed the bird will be quite clean inside, and need only wiping with a wet cloth; if not clean, pour lukewarm water *through* the bird, wipe inside and out with a towel, but do not *wash* the outside unless necessary from accidental soiling. With care, a chicken may be emptied without any uncleanliness; lay the bird aside.

The gall, a small dark green bladder, is attached to the liver; cut it off, leaving a bit of the liver with it to avoid breaking, throw the liver into cold water; by cutting the gizzard very carefully at the wide side without penetrating the inner skin, it can be peeled off, leaving the inside whole, thus avoiding the usual mess made by inexperienced hands. Scald and skin the feet (see directions, page 47); put liver, gizzard, heart, feet and neck on in a pint of water, if chicken or duck; a quart, if turkey, with a slice of onion and piece of carrot if at hand, and let them stew slowly down to half the quantity, when they will be a stiff jelly.

TO TRUSS AND STUFF CHICKEN OR TURKEY.—For roasting, twist the pinions under the wing to the back, push up the legs till they lie flat against the side of the bird and the lower joints are even with the rump; pass a skewer through the centre of the thighs bringing it out opposite, fasten them in that position with a cord, fasten the ends of the legs close to the vent; press on the breast bone hard with the palm of the hand. If the bird is to be stuffed, loosen the skin of the breast and put the forcemeat (see recipe) where the crop was, turn the neck skin over to the back and sew it.

ROAST CHICKEN.

Flour it, set it in a dripping-pan with a few slices of fat pork laid on the breast, or else put a few pieces of butter on it. If you do not use the pork, put an ounce of butter in a wooden spoon, press it to make it stick; to baste, rub the butter side over the bird; keep the spoon in a cool spot when not in use.

Allow fifteen minutes to the pound, turn the chicken over when the one side is brown; when done take it up. If you used pork, pour off the fat and remove the pork; have the gizzard ready chopped, the liver mashed fine, and a teaspoonful of flour mixed with it; pour the liquor from the giblets to it, stir well, then pour the whole into the pan and boil it on the stove.

Take the string and skewers from the chicken, set it in a dish, with watercress round it, pour the gravy in a tureen and serve.

ROAST FOWL.

If the fowl is over a year old, wrap it in two coats of soft paper after it is prepared as above; set it in the oven, allowing an hour and a half in a good oven; when it has been in an hour, take off the paper and let it brown. This method of semi-steaming it will make it tender; make gravy and serve as in last recipe.

FOWL BRAISED.

Loosely fill a nice fowl with forcemeat; put it in a stewpan with a pint of broth, two glasses of white wine, an onion stuck with two cloves, a piece of carrot to make half a cup when cut up, a blade of mace, half a teaspoon of salt, a quarter of pepper; lay thin slices of pork over the fowl and cover the pot closely; let it cook *very gently* one hour from the time it begins to boil; take the fowl from the pot and put it in the oven to brown; strain the gravy into a smaller saucepan and boil it down fast till it is a glaze, or looks like syrup; glaze the fowl with this (see Glazing, p. 32) when it is brown. Have ready a can of mushrooms stewed with their liquor ten minutes in the liquor from the giblets; thicken this with brown thickening.

If you have no broth or stock to braise the fowl, you must have made it with the giblets beforehand, and use only brown sauce to stew the mushrooms in.

ROAST TURKEY.

Except in point of time, follow the directions for roasting chicken. For stuffing, see directions for trussing and stuffing turkey. On account of the length of time it requires to be in the oven, a turkey should be covered with well-buttered paper for the first half the time. It will take three hours to cook a moderate-sized one; it must be very frequently basted and turned about. Dish and serve as chicken, except that it should be garnished with sausages fried brown, or fried oysters. The latter is the more elegant mode, especially if it is stuffed with oysters (see Forcemeats).

BRAISED TURKEY.

"Turkey braised, the Lord be praised," is part of an old saying which at all events testifies to the estimation in which our forefathers held this mode of preparing the savory bird.

Cover the turkey with slices of pork, tying it round with cord to keep it in shape. Put four slices of pork in the pot or braising pan; put the turkey stuffed on these; lay the giblets round it, with four onions, three cloves, three carrots cut small, a parsnip, two bay leaves, a bouquet of herbs (see Bouquet), a teaspoonful of salt, and half of pepper, and almost cover this with any good stock you may have. Cover tightly and allow to simmer very gently from four to six hours, according to the size of the bird. Braised turkey is served hot or cold; if it is to be eaten hot let it be in the oven to brown, unless you have cooked it in a regular braising-pan which will hold hot coals on the lid, when the oven will be unnecessary; remove the vegetables, boil the gravy down rapidly, skimming it to free it from fat. Garnish either with carrot and turnip cut into fancy forms and boiled separately, or with small sausages fried. Strain part of the gravy, stir in a spoonful of brown thickening, and pour it over the bird.

If it is to be served cold, let it remain in the gravy in which it was braised for an hour after it leaves the fire; then strain the liquor; boil down to two-thirds its original quantity, so that when cold it will form a hard jelly; free it from fat; clear with white of egg (see directions for clearing stock); brush two coats of this over the turkey and let the rest get cold; when stiff cut it into stars or strips, chopping the trimmings of it and use to garnish the dish.

BOILED TURKEY.

Prepare a turkey as directed. In trussing turkey for boiling, the legs are pushed up, a slit cut in each side, and the legs drawn into the body; it is correct to stuff the breast for roasting, but for boiling the inside may be filled with oyster forcemeat (see recipe) or with chestnuts; bind it into shape with tape, flour it, put it into an oval pot with just warm water enough to cover it; put in a dessert-spoonful of salt, a carrot, an onion, and four cloves, and a dozen pepper-corns, a few sticks of celery, and a bouquet of herbs; bring it to a boil; simmer a turkey of ten pounds very gently for two hours after it reaches the boiling point, skim off every bit of scum as it rises or it will discolor the bird. Take it up, drain it a moment, make some thick white sauce or béchamel (see recipe) with some of the water it was boiled in, pour it over the turkey to mask it. Send to table with it either oyster sauce, celery sauce, or Hollandaise, or even good parsley sauce. Garnish with forcemeat balls, or little rolls of crisp bacon, or lemon and parsley.

BOILED CHICKEN is cooked in the same way, but allowing half the time or less if small, and half the ingredients in the water.

ROAST DUCK OR GOOSE.

Clean a duck as directed for fowls; twist the pinions round on the back; it is correct English fashion to leave the feet on; scald them, and twist them up against the back. If you prefer them off, however, break the bone below the joint, and cut them off. Stuff the body of the duck with forcemeat (see forcemeat for ducks), sew up the slit and press the legs close to the side of the bird, securing them with a skewer and cord.

Many people like duck underdone; when this is so, half an hour in a hot oven will cook a quite young one; the usual time for a duck weighing four pounds is one hour. Make brown gravy in the dripping-pan with the stock from the giblets, chopping the liver and gizzard, and skimming off all grease, let this boil down until rich and brown. Send hot apple sauce to table with the duck.

A goose is cooked and trussed exactly as duck, excepting that in no case should the feet of a goose be left on. The time for a young goose is one hour and a half; it should be frequently basted, and served very brown. If the skin is very fat and oily, some prefer to parboil the bird half an hour in salt and water; then flour it, and put it in a very hot oven, or it will not brown; once it begins to color, the heat may be a little slackened; serve with brown giblet sauce and apple sauce in separate tureens.

ROAST CAPON.

Follow the directions for roast turkey. If wanted for a company dinner, it may be stuffed with chestnut forcemeat (see recipe), and served on a bed of watercresses.

CHAPTER XXVIII.

GAME.

As much as the French excel the English in soups and all made dishes, so do the latter excel them in roasts and game.

The English rule for game is to leave the natural flavor unimpaired; therefore they use no forcemeat, no flavored sauces, no larding, butter only is used to baste, and that liberally, and bread sauce which has little flavor of its own, but is said to bring out that of game, is served with it.

Therefore in the following recipes where I have prescribed pork, I am following French or American taste; but it may always be replaced by butter, *I* think, to advantage.

ROAST GROUSE, PRAIRIE HEN, OR PARTRIDGE.

Clean as directed for poultry in general. If you wish to serve these birds English fashion, instead of cutting the head off, make a slit to take out the crop, and twist the head round and bring it under the wing; rub the breast and legs with lemon, then mix a teaspoonful of salt, a quarter one of white pepper, and a tablespoonful of butter together, put them inside the bird; take a slice of fat pork, broad and long, and lay it over the breast and legs; truss the bird into good shape with skewers and twine, and roll it in buttered paper. Put in a dripping-pan in a quick oven, leave it half an hour; then take off the paper, dredge the bird with flour lightly, and baste thoroughly, put it in a part of the oven where it will brown quickly. When a good color take it up, remove strings and skewers, but not the slices of pork; put a little stock or boiling water in the dripping-pan stirring well, skim off the grease, then squeeze in the juice of half an orange, add a little pepper and salt, and serve with bread sauce.

BROILED PRAIRIE HEN, OR PARTRIDGE.

Clean and prepare as directed. Split the back of the bird, butter it all over, place it on a hot gridiron and turn several times to prevent burning. It will take, on a good fire, fifteen to twenty minutes, according to size; just before it is done, sprinkle with salt and pepper. While the bird is cooking, chop a teaspoonful of parsley very fine, mix it with the juice of a quarter lemon and a tablespoonful of butter. This quantity is for each bird, put this *maître d'hotel butter*, as it is called, on a very hot dish, and lay the bird first on paper to take any dark grease there may be, and than lay it on the dish; garnish with parsley.

ANOTHER WAY (BLOT),

And preferred by me, is as follows: Split each bird in two lengthwise pieces; put butter the size of an egg in a stewpan, set it on a good fire, when hot lay the birds in; leave them till about half cooked, turning them three or four times; then take them off, put them on a gridiron, cook fifteen minutes and serve with the following sauce: Put with the butter in the stewpan in which were the birds, a teaspoonful of chopped parsley, one of chopped mushrooms, salt and pepper; sprinkle in, and stir at same time, a teaspoonful of flour, a gill of white wine, and one of broth, boil till slightly thick; serve the birds on it, or they may be served with mayonnaise sauce.

SALMI OF GAME.

See salmi of duck, and follow directions.

ROAST QUAILS.

These, being birds of white flesh, are unlike most game, which is better kept long after killing, and should be cooked *very fresh*. Clean the birds; roll each in a thin slice of salt pork, tying it on with cord; lay the birds on a dripping-pan, and baste often; when done, serve on slices of toasted or fried bread, with the crust cut off.

BROILED QUAILS.

Cook exactly the same as partridge, only of course they require much less time to cook, ten minutes usually suffices; serve on toast, with watercresses round the dish.

SMALL BIRDS, SNIPE, WOODCOCK, ETC.

Leave on the head and neck, carefully picked free of feathers; twist the head, and use the beaks of snipe and woodcock as a skewer to secure the legs, running it through the body; wrap each one in bacon, fastened with wooden toothpicks, and put them in a hot oven. Have as many slices of bread, cut round, and fried brown in butter as you have birds; when done (they will not take more than twelve or fifteen minutes in a hot oven), place each on a slice of bread, and serve very hot.

A QUICK WAY TO COOK SMALL BIRDS.

Prepare them as usual; dip each bird in flour and shake them; sprinkle with salt. Have a kettle with smoking lard; try it with a piece of bread, if it colors brown in one-half minute it is ready, if not wait and try again. When it is hot enough drop the birds in; they will cool the lard, therefore don't put in more than six at a time; three minutes will cook them; try the lard before putting in more. Have ready as many rounds of bread as you have birds, soaked in egg and milk—two eggs to half a pint; drain each piece and drop them into the hot fat; take them up when pale brown and lay a bird on each.

If the fire is good and the fat deep enough (there should be two to three pounds in the kettle), a dozen birds and a dozen rounds of bread will take less than twenty minutes, and make a most delicious dish.

Epicures prefer that woodcock and snipe should not be drawn, but the entrails—otherwise the "trail"—be caught on toast laid under them in cooking.

ROAST VENISON.

Trim neatly a well-hung haunch of venison, scraping off all dark skin and dried surface; wipe thoroughly, and if it is getting "high" let the cloths be dipped in vinegar; cover the haunch with a thick sheet of white cartridge paper well buttered; tie this securely over. Baste the venison to prevent the paper from burning; half an hour before the meat is done remove the paper, sprinkle a little salt over the meat, dredge it with flour, and baste liberally with butter stuck in a spoon. Pour the fat from the dripping-pan, keeping back any brown gravy there may be; pour a cup of boiling water to this, and boil it down adding only salt; serve the gravy in a tureen; put a frill of white paper round the knuckle, and serve very hot. Allow fifteen minutes to the pound. Red-currant jelly and venison sauce should be served with venison. Venison sauce is equal parts of mutton broth, made very strong, and port wine, with a little cayenne pepper. Many simply serve currant jelly made hot.

Some roast the haunch in a flour-and-water paste until nearly done, when it is removed and the meat browned.

VENISON CUTLETS OR STEAKS.

Cut cutlets or steaks an inch thick, trim neatly, but take away no fat; pepper and salt them; broil them on a hot gridiron over a clear, gentle fire; turn often, they will take twenty minutes; send stewed mushrooms and baked potatoes to table with them; or, if you have no mushrooms, make some currant jelly hot, and send it as sauce.

CHAPTER XXIX.

SALADS.

Although there are many salads of different names, there are but two dressings in ordinary use: the simple French dressing, suitable for any salad where there is no meat used, and mayonnaise. There are many others, of course, several varieties of *English* dressing all more or less bad—American dressings no better.

The French excel in salads, and it is rare, indeed, at a French table to eat one poorly mixed. Yet their method is very simple, so simple, indeed, that many think it cannot matter in mixing oil and vinegar whether one or other goes first, provided the quantities are right; but this is the secret, the oil *must be first*. The reason is this: if the leaves are wet first with the vinegar, the oil will not adhere and will lay at the bottom of the bowl, and a sharp, crude salad will be the result. This shows, too, why the lettuce must always be *well dried* before being put in the bowl.

LETTUCE SALAD.

This is best prepared on the table, as it should be eaten soon after it is made.

The lettuce should be carefully washed and dried. Hold over the bowl a salad-spoon, into which put a saltspoonful of salt and a quarter one of white pepper;

then fill the salad-spoon with oil; pour this over the lettuce, and toss the leaves over and over till they shine; then put two more tablespoonfuls of oil, toss it again; then put one tablespoonful of vinegar; mix lightly, and the salad is made. These are average proportions; many like four parts oil to one of vinegar.

ANCHOVY SALAD.

Wash six anchovies; let them lie in water an hour; remove the bones, also heads, fins and tails; put them on a dish with two lettuces, a teaspoonful of chopped parsley, and a sliced lemon; pour over them either a simple French dressing or a mayonnaise sauce (see recipe).

CARDINAL SALAD.

Take two or three heads of very white celery, using only the best part; cut them of even lengths; place them on a flat dish, arranging them like a bundle of asparagus, taking care that some of the delicate leaves are at each end; color some thick mayonnaise with lobster coral pounded, or with red beetroot boiled tender and rubbed through a sieve—using enough of either to make the same a bright red; pour it in spoonfuls over the middle of the celery until it is entirely masked, leaving the pale green ends untouched by the sauce. Put it on the ice till needed for use.

ASPARAGUS SALAD.

Take cold asparagus that has been boiled twenty minutes—that is till tender, but not in a mush; color some mayonnaise, green, either with spinach (see Spinach Coloring) or juice of bruised parsley. Arrange the asparagus neatly in a pile on a dish, all the heads one way; put it on the ice till very cold; then pour over it the green mayonnaise (which must not be thin enough to run off), leaving the asparagus points, however, untouched. This is an excellent breakfast salad.

CHICKEN SALAD, (SOYER'S).

If you can make a good mayonnaise, chicken salad is very easy to make, yet seldom well made. Cut up the chickens quite small, make a plain French dressing (three tablespoonfuls of oil to one of vinegar, salt and pepper), pour it over the chicken, and leave it an hour; take as much celery cut up small as you have chicken, and toss both together, taking care to remember that the salad ought to be seasoned sufficiently before the mayonnaise is put on; then make a mound as smooth as possible and cover it with mayonnaise which has been on ice till very firm; dip a knife in water to smooth it. Ornament either with celery tops alone or with capers, stoned olives, gherkins or hard egg.

If lettuce is used instead of celery treat the chicken as before, but lay the lettuce leaves round the dish.

LOBSTER SALAD.

Take a live hen lobster, plunge its head downwards in boiling water; this kills it instantly; be sure the water is salt enough; two large tablespoonfuls to the gallon of water is not too much; boil it slowly twenty-five minutes if medium size, if large, half an hour; if over boiled, the lobster will be tough. Put it into cold water when done for one minute, then break the shell and crack the claws. Take away the sand bag from the head, the entrail that runs through the tail and the spongy parts that lie just under the shell. Save the coral, any eggs there may be under the tail, the white fat that adheres to the shell, and the green fat in the body. Cut the lobster into dice, or tear it with two forks; pour upon it just enough French dressing to moisten and season it, or mayonnaise may be used. This may be done some time before the salad is eaten, but the putting together must be done the last thing; this is true of all salads; lay crisp white lettuce leaves or celery in the dish; lay on them the lobster, and the green and white fat; pour over it a mayonnaise; garnish with olives and the lobster claws; separate the eggs and sprinkle them over the salad dressing, or use the coral chopped if there are no eggs.

Veal or lean roast pork when very tender and well cooked, dressed precisely in the same way as chicken salad, are exceedingly good, although they should never be used as a substitute for chicken in so-called "chicken salad." On their own merits they would meet approval, while under a false name they may be scorned.

POTATO SALAD.

Boil the potatoes *in their skins* till tender but not broken; peal and slice them while warm; let them get cold but not ice cold; chop a teaspoonful of onion or olives very fine; throw it over them and pour over them French dressing enough to moisten them well.

Potatoes boiled in their skins are less likely to break than when peeled beforehand.

This is the usual way of making potato salad; but I prefer it made in the following manner:

POTATO MAYONNAISE.

Boil potatoes in their skins, peel and slice them as

above. Make mayonnaise sauce, chop a small onion very fine indeed, mix it with the mayonnaise, and dress the potatoes with it; garnish with tufts of parsley.

BREAKFAST SALAD, (MURREY).

Scald two ripe tomatoes, take off the skin, put them into cold water or on ice; drain and either slice them, or cut them into sections as you would divide an orange; peel and slice very thin one cucumber; put in a salad bowl a few leaves of Romaine lettuce, add the tomatoes and cucumber, one spring onion cut up, and, if possible, a few tarragon-leaves; pour over the salad a plain salad dressing.

TOMATO SALAD.

Scald and skin fine ripe tomatoes; cut them either in slices or in sections parallel to the core, leaving the hard core out; set them on the ice till very cold; pour over them either a mayonnaise or a French dressing.

TOMATO SALAD, NO. 2.

Scald some tomatoes, choosing round ones; skin them; let them get firm on ice; wash some fresh lettuce; put two or three young leaves in a saucer, using as many saucers as there are persons at table. Slice each tomato neatly and put the slices so that the tomato appears uncut. Set one on each saucer in the middle of the lettuce leaves; put on each a dessert-spoonful of mayonnaise sauce.

CHAPTER XXX.

BOILED PUDDINGS OF ALL KINDS.

They must be put in boiling water and brought back to the boiling point as *quickly* as possible; not allowed to boil again, just whenever is most convenient; steeping a pudding in non-boiling water ruins it. Then it must boil *every minute* of the time directed, and should the water boil away too much, be replenished from a kettle of *boiling* water. This will hardly be necessary, however, if the pudding was well covered with water at first, except in the case of those requiring to boil more than two hours, such as Christmas puddings, etc.

ENGLISH APPLE, OR OTHER FRUIT PUDDING

The English use a beef-suet crust where Americans use a biscuit crust, and as it is both more wholesome and more nutritious, I give the recipe hoping that those who shudder at the idea of suet pastry will give it a trial. It is no more trouble to make than biscuit dough.

Get *beef kidney* suet; take all the skin from half a pound of it; chop it very fine; put in a small teaspoonful of salt; mix it with a scant pound of flour; make a hole in the centre and put in a small cup of water; mix it as quickly and as lightly as you would biscuit; add more water, if needed, to make it a *firm* but not hard paste; roll out on a floured board once to the thickness of half an inch; butter a quart bowl well; line it with this paste, pressing it in every part *lightly;* leave it an inch above the bowl; cut off what remains over the inch margin; roll it out for the cover; then fill the bowl with apples peeled and cut in slices; heap it up high; pour over them as much sugar as you think your apples will need, and grate the rind of a lemon or some nutmeg over them; pour in half a cup of water; wet the edge of the paste, put on the cover, pinch the edges together; see that the water cannot get out; then flour a cloth; cover the top of the pudding with it; pass a string round the bowl outside the cloth half-way down (so that the flare of the bowl will prevent the string if well tied from slipping up); tie the four corners of the pudding cloth over the top of the bowl, so that you can lift the pudding by it; then put it into a pot of fast-boiling water—which must be kept boiling, and if it diminishes much, replenish from another kettle kept boiling. Serve with hard sauce.

RASPBERRY PUDDING is made in the same way, using three parts of raspberries and one of currants in place of the apples.

CHERRY PUDDING, with the same proportion of currants, is a delicious pudding.

FRUIT BATTER PUDDING.

Make a batter with four eggs, and a pint of flour and a pinch of salt, using as much milk as will make a rather thick batter; stir in as many raspberries or cherries as you can, with half a cupful of sugar. Serve with hard sauce or a sauce of the fruit (see Fruit Sauce).

ALBERT PUDDING.

Beat six ounces of butter to a cream; then gradually add to it five well-beaten eggs and half a pound of flour, six ounces of loaf-sugar, the rind of a lemon grated; add half a pound of stoned raisins; butter a bowl or mould thickly, ornament it with stars and diamonds of citron and figs; pour the mixture in a bowl which it must fill within half an inch; cover with a cloth as directed for apple pudding. Boil or steam it at least three hours.

LEMON PUDDING.

Twelve ounces of bread-crumbs, six ounces of finely-chopped beef suet, four ounces of flour, four ounces of sugar, the grated peel and juice of two small lemons, four eggs; mix all together, and then add milk enough to make a thick batter. Boil in a buttered bowl or mould three hours and a half. If a bowl is used, cover with a floured cloth and tie up as directed for apple pudding. Sift sugar over it when done. Serve with lemon or wine sauce.

POLKA PUDDING.

Boil one quart of milk; mix four tablespoonfuls of cornstarch with a little cold milk, and pour the boiling milk on to it, stirring all the time; let it thicken over the fire; then add two tablespoonfuls of rose or orange-flower water (*I* find this rather too much, begin with one, then taste). Stir in, either three tablespoonfuls of rich cream or three ounces of butter; blanch one ounce of bitter almonds, two of sweet, and beat them up quite fine, using white of one egg to prevent oiling; beat the yolk with three other whole eggs well, and add them to the mixture; stir all over the fire till thick and smooth; put in a mould and ice it. Serve with polka sauce (see recipe). Sauce *boiling hot*, pudding *cold*, on *hot* plates.

QUEEN MAB PUDDING.

Steep six bitter almonds bruised, and the peel of a lemon (pared *very* thin) in a pint of milk on the stove, at almost boiling point, until the flavor is well drawn out; add one ounce of gelatine and a pinch of salt; stir till gelatine is dissolved; strain and return to the saucepan; add half a pint of thick cream and five ounces of sugar; let it all just boil; stir in quickly the yolks of six eggs well beaten; set the saucepan in boiling water and stir till thick, but be careful not to let the eggs curdle; pour it out and stir till nearly cold; then mix two and a half ounces of candied cherries, and two ounces of citron cut small; or three ounces of preserved ginger, and one ounce of pistache nuts blanched; pour the pudding into an oiled mould and pack in ice. If ginger is used, serve the ginger syrup as a sauce; if cherries, use cherry syrup or currant jelly mixed with syrup for sauce; boil together half a cup of water and a cup of sugar to make the syrup.

TROY PUDDING.

This is an excellent plain pudding; one cup of chopped and seeded raisins, one cup of suet finely chopped, one cup of molasses, one cup of milk, three eggs, three cups of flour, one teaspoonful of soda; spice to taste, saltspoonful of salt; mix all the dry ingredients first; then put molasses, the eggs well beaten, and the milk ; boil three hours in a buttered bowl. Serve with good wine or lemon sauce.

ENGLISH CHRISTMAS PUDDINGS

There are many good recipes differing very little from each other, any one of which would make as good a pudding as usually met with in "old England," but it requires more than a good recipe to turn out the pudding as it is eaten there; the best recipe is more often than not spoiled in the cooking. I have known them to be three-parts boiled (as is the usual way) and given to friends, and yet in the final two hours' boiling be spoiled.

In the tying up and boiling lies the art of making any good boiled pudding; bear in mind the bowl or pudding boiler must be *full*, the cloth tied firmly over the bowl (it will always "give" enough for the swelling of the pudding), the water be fast boiling, and when the pudding is put in, be quickly brought to the boil again, and kept boiling every minute of the time prescribed, replenishing from a kettle of boiling water kept for that purpose. If the pudding ceases to boil you will find it sticky.

The orthodox Christmas pudding is always an equal quantity of suet, fruit and eggs; the variations are in the proportions of ingredients added for flavoring, and in the flour some families (and it is usually a family recipe handed down for generations), use the same proportion of flour as of each kind of fruit, others use half flour and half bread-crumbs, others again use all bread-crumbs and no flour. I give three recipes, all excellent, provided they are properly boiled.

CHRISTMAS PUDDING, NO. 1.

One pound of currants thoroughly cleaned, one pound of raisins, stoned and chopped a little, one pound of suet finely chopped, half a pound of brown sugar, four ounces of blanched almonds split, four ounces of citron, four of candied lemon peel, four of candied orange peel, one pound of flour and eight eggs, two glasses of brandy, and milk to make all into a very thick batter just so that you can stir it. A teaspoonful of salt scant, and a small nutmeg grated, a teaspoonful of ginger, a scant one of cinnamon and half one of cloves, all ground.

CHRISTMAS PUDDING, NO. 2 (VERY RICH).

This is a very delicious pudding, richer than the other.

One pound of Muscatel raisins stoned, half pound of Sultana raisins, half a pound of currants, half a pound of mixed candied peels, half a nutmeg grated, three-quarters of a pound of bread-crumbs, three-quarters of a pound of beef suet chopped very fine, ten eggs, a quarter an ounce of *bitter* almonds pounded, one tablespoonful of flour, four ounces brown sugar, a gill of brandy and one of sherry.

N. B.—In both these puddings the spices may be increased or lessened, the candied peels varied or part omitted. These are matters of taste, and do not affect the texture or character of the pudding.

TO MIX PLUM PUDDING.

Throw each ingredient as you prepare it into a pan; sprinkle the salt over all, then add the beaten eggs, the brandy, and when milk is used, put that last, as it is only when the eggs and brandy are in you can tell how much you need. The mixture must be so stiff as to stir with difficulty. In the last recipe the bitter almonds must be crumbled and added by degrees with great care.

The quantities given make two quart puddings, or may be boiled in one.

If boiled in two, use quart bowls; butter them well, fill them, put a buttered paper over the top, scald a pudding cloth, flour it, tie it over (see general directions for puddings), and boil each pudding six hours; and two hours on the day used. If one large pudding is made, boil eight hours, and two on the day used.

These puddings may also be boiled in cloths (many consider them lighter so boiled). Scald and flour a square of muslin for each; lay it in a large bowl; pour the pudding mixture in, tie it up closely as you would dumplings, and boil six hours for a quart pudding, and an hour and half the day used.

CHAPTER XXXI.

PIES AND TARTS.

In making either the American pie, or the English tart, remember to heap the fruit in the centre, leaving room for a groove round the edge. Before the cover is put on wet the margin, but do not press the *edges* together, all the pressure should come between the fruit and the edge—lay your forefinger round, pressing closely so that upper and under paste may adhere there, but leave the edges untouched; cut four slits in the groove you have made; see that they are open enough for the syrup to boil into the groove instead of from the edges and out in the oven; as the pie cools the syrup runs back from the groove to the pie. See full directions in Chapter III, for Pastry.

FLAKY CRUST FOR FAMILY PIES.

South Kensington Training School of Cookery.

Put one pound of flour in a bowl, mix with it a teaspoonful of baking powder, whip the whites of two eggs to a stiff foam, put them to the flour with a scant saltspoonful of salt, and make all into a stiff paste with ice-cold water (about one gill).

Flour a board, turn the paste out on it; flour the rolling-pin, and roll it to a thin sheet. Divide half a pound of butter into three parts. Take one part and spread it all over the paste with a knife, dredge flour over it and fold the paste in three, flour the rolling-pin again, roll out the paste and spread the second portion of butter over it; fold the paste as before, roll it out and spread the third portion of butter. Fold it again and roll it to the thickness required for a pie—the third of an inch.

This paste requires a quick oven.

ENGLISH FRUIT TARTS.

These are made in oval deep dishes, with crust only lining the sides, not the bottom, giving more fruit and juice, and are preferred by those who do not like the heavy undercrust.

CURRANT AND RASPBERRY TARTS.

Cut long strips of "rough puff paste" (see recipe) an inch and half to two inches wide, wet the sides of an oval dish, lay the paste round, pressing the sides not the edges—fill with three parts raspberries, one of currants, pour in a cup of water and one of sugar, wetting margin and put on a cover, observing directions (Pastry, Chapter III).

CHERRY AND CURRANT TART.

Use three parts cherries and one of currants, unless you have regular cooking cherries, when the currants may not be necessary, make the tart according to directions for raspberry and currant tart.

BLACKBERRY TART.

Blackberry tarts or pies are greatly improved by having one-third apple added to them. Make as directed for other fruit tarts.

APPLE and all fruit tarts are made in the same way.

APPLE PIE.

Make some "rough puff paste" (see recipe); roll half of it thin; line a pie-plate; peel and cut up some fine baking apples; fill the pie (see Chapter III). Grate the rind of a lemon or some nutmeg over it; put two tablespoonfuls of sugar, or more if apples are tart, and half a cup of water over it; roll out the rest of the paste for cover, the third of an inch thick, and cover as directed elsewhere.

APPLE PIE, NO. 2.

Make some very nice apple sauce—which must be long and slowly stewed till it is almost jelly; flavor with lemon peel and a little juice; line a pie-plate with "rough puff" paste; cut some strips an inch and half wide, lay this round the edge over the lining so as to make a double edge, pressing only the lower part of the strip; pour in the apple sauce, which must be *cool;* sift sugar over thickly; cut thin strips of the paste, twist them and lay them over in cross-bars; in every open square stick half a blanched almond if wanted ornamental, or else after it is baked a saltspoonful of red jelly in every square opening.

This pie may be made with any preserve.

LEMON PIE, NO. 1.

Beat two ounces of butter to a cream, if very salt wash it first, mix with it four ounces of sugar, a cup of bread-crumbs and the yolks of three eggs and one white, the grated rind of two lemons, the juice of one. Stir briskly and pour into a pie-plate lined with paste, bake in a moderate oven; beat two heaping tablespoonfuls of powdered sugar with the whites of two eggs, make a meringue and cover the pie with it; return to the oven to color.

LEMON PIE, NO. 2.

Two teaspoonfuls of corn-starch mixed with six of cold water; stir a scant cup of boiling water in it and boil, stirring all the while, just as you would make starch; when it has boiled five minutes, grate the rind of two lemons to it, add five ounces of sugar and the juice of the lemons, two ounces of butter, stirring the latter in one way till the mixture boils, then let cool one minute, beat in the yolks of four eggs the whites of two, stir well two minutes, then pour the mixture into two medium-sized pie-plates. Bake in a moderate oven.

Beat the whites of two eggs with two heaping tablespoonfuls of powdered sugar, spread it over the pie when it comes out of the oven; return it, and let the meringue color lightly.

LEMON PIE, NO. 3 (RICH).

Take four ounces of stale cup or sponge cake, or the same quantity of macaroons, crumbled; squeeze over the crumbs the juice of three lemons, grate the rind of two; three-quarters of a pint of rich cream, or six ounces of butter beaten to cream, and a quarter of a pound of sugar; pour over these ingredients the well-beaten yolks of six eggs, and the whites of three; add a small pinch of salt and mix.

Pour the mixture into two medium pie-dishes lined with rough puff paste (see recipe). Use the three whites left for meringue which spread over the pies.

COCOANUT PIE, NO. 1.

Line a dish with rough puff paste, pour a pint of hot milk (not boiling) over two well beaten eggs; set the bowl containing the mixture in boiling water, stir it till thick, then take it out, and stir in half a cup of sugar, and either a cup of grated cocoanut, or a cup of dessicated cocoanut, with a teaspoonful of vanilla or the grated rind of half a lemon.

COCOANUT PIE, NO. 2.

Mix two eggs well beaten with a cup of milk and the milk of the nut, if it is quite sweet; take off the brown skin of the nut, and grate it as finely as possible; mix with it three tablespoonfuls of bread-crumbs, three tablespoonfuls of sifted sugar, two ounces of butter beaten to cream, six ounces of Muscatel raisins stoned and chopped and the grated rind of a lemon; mix and fill the pies, bake in a moderate oven thoroughly.

This also makes a good boiled pudding.

SWEET PATTIES.

Take a pound of fine puff or rough puff paste; roll it the third of an inch thick, and cut with a biscuit cutter three rounds; put one on the other; then with a smaller biscuit cutter dipped in flour press on the top, cutting only one-third through. When you have as many as you want, glaze with white of egg; bake them in a quick oven. These are the shells to be filled with jam or preserve, and will rise to three inches. Delicious patties are simply filled with thick cream twenty-four hours' old, sweetened, flavored with vanilla and whipped till firm; when prepared as directed above, remove the centre piece of the patties, which is the cover, scoop out the soft dough, leaving half an inch of crust; put the cream or preserve in with a spoon, pile it high, and lay on the cover.

FRANGIPANI CREAM PATTIES.

Prepare the pastry shells as directed; take off the centre piece, which is the cover; scoop out the soft inside, leaving half an inch of crust, and fill with Frangipani cream, made as follows:

One gill of cream, one tablespoonful of flour, one tablespoonful of orange flour water, two of brandy or one of sherry and one of brandy, mix and put in a small saucepan, boil till the mixture leaves the sides of the pan; if it becomes thicker than very thick cream, add more cream or milk; beat in the yolks of four eggs, six macaroons crumbled, four tablespoonfuls of sugar, the peel of a lemon grated and a tablespoonful of any candied fruit, or ginger or citron, cut *very fine;* set the saucepan in boiling water after the eggs are added, and stir till very thick; when cool it is ready for use. It will keep a long time if put into jars and covered with buttered paper.

TARTLETS.

As these need not rise so much, you can use the trimmings from patties to make them. Roll the paste quite thin; double it without rolling it again, and cover patty pans with it, pressing the bottom as thin as you can, but not the sides or edges; cut pieces of bread the size of the bottom of the patty pans and put one in each. Bake in a quick oven. When done take out the bread and put jam or preserve in its place. You may, when cool, if you choose, put a spoonful of stiff whipped cream on them; or instead of the jam fill them with frangipani cream. In this case only let them color very lightly in the oven, and when filled with the cream return them to the oven to brown.

OMELETTE SOUFFLÉE. (JULES GOUFFÉ.)

The whites of six eggs beaten very stiff; the yolks of three beaten four minutes, with three tablespoonfuls of sugar powdered, and one teaspoonful of vanilla extract or the powdered vanilla which is better; turn the whites on to the yolks and mix very gently, lifting the yolks as it were, *over* the whites till blended, yet not *stirring* them at all; butter an oval dish—a soufflée pan is best, but an earthen or thick tin will do; turn the mixture very lightly into it; sift sugar over, and bake in a moderate oven till a golden brown. Serve instantly or it will fall.

SOUFFLÉE A LA VANILLE. (J. GOUFFÉ.)

Put in a three-quart saucepan one quart of milk, keeping little of it out to mix with six ounces of flour; when smooth stir the flour into the milk; keep on stirring till it boils, when take it off the fire at once; put in six ounces of sugar, two teaspoonfuls of vanilla powder or extract, and a pinch of salt; break six eggs, add the yolks to the paste, one at a time, beating it well; beat the whites very stiff, and add them very *gently* to the rest; if quickly done, the whites go to liquid, and the paste becomes too wet.

Bake for twenty minutes in a buttered pan.

FLAMING OMELETTE.

Break six eggs; beat the whites and yolks separately; add to the yolks one tablespoonful of powdered sugar; stir whites and yolks lightly together; put butter the size of an egg in a clean frying-pan, let it get hot and begin to boil; then pour the omelette in; lift the pan on one side for a minute, then let the mixture that is not set, run over to the other side, detach the omelette with a spoon from the side of the pan; when it is partly set, shake the pan gently back and forth to loosen it; turn it half over with a cake turner; slip it on a hot dish, dust over with sugar, and pour over it six tablespoonfuls of rum—warmed if the weather is cold; set it alight and serve flaming.

This omelette may be made as directed in Part First, if preferred.

CHAPTER XXXII.

DISHES FOR CHEESE COURSE, OR FOR SUPPER.

CHEESE FONDUE.

Put in a small saucepan one tablespoonful of butter, one of flour; stir over the fire till they bubble; then add a gill of milk or cream (so far this is only very thick white sauce); stir to prevent burning; when smooth stir into it three ounces of finely-grated cheese of fine quality, a saltspoonful (scant) of salt, and a tiny pinch of cayenne; turn it when well mixed into a bowl and stir into it the beaten yolks of two eggs; thoroughly whisk the whites of *three* eggs solid; stir them in very gently the last thing. Butter a dish or tin which the fondue will half fill, as it rises very much; bake till golden brown in a quick oven; pin a *hot* napkin around the dish in which it is baked; serve instantly or it will fall.

RAMINOLES (SOYER).

Melt one tablespoonful of butter; add one of floor; stir over the fire till they bubble; add half a cup of water, stir in four ounces of cheese grated; stir till smooth; remove from the fire; stir in, very gradually, three eggs well beaten; have ready a buttered baking-sheet and drop the mixture on it in lumps the size of a walnut; press each slightly on top; brush them over with beaten egg; put a spoonful of grated cheese in the depression, and bake in a hot oven twelve minutes. Serve hot as possible.

RAMAQUINS.

Crumble a slice of stale baker's bread; cover it with a breakfast cup of boiling milk; let it soak a quarter of an hour in a hot place; then strain off the milk but don't press it; beat it smooth; stir in it two ounces of butter which the warm bread will melt, then four ounces of grated cheese (half parmesan is best), half a teaspoonful of made mustard, half a teaspoonful of sifted sugar, half a saltspoonful of pepper, one of salt, as much powdered mace as will go on the end of a penknife, and the yolks of three eggs; mix together thoroughly; just before you are ready to bake them beat the whites of four eggs solid; stir them into the mixture; either have buttered paper soufflée cases ready to bake them in, or deep patty pans lined with puff paste; only half fill them; they will take ten to fifteen minutes to bake in pastry, six to ten in paper. Have a hot oven and serve very hot.

CHEESE STRAWS.

Make some puff paste or "rough puff"; roll it out as thick as a silver dollar; cut it in strips an inch and a half wide and four inches long; lay a little *rich* grated cheese along the centre of half the strips; then on each lay a strip without cheese, thus making a sandwich as it were; brush each one over with the yolk of egg; bake in a quick oven; serve cold or warm, piled on a napkin, blockhouse fashion, with mustard and cress or parsley garnish.

CHEESE CANOPÉES.

Cut some stale baker's bread into slices half an inch thick; if you have a half-moon shaped cutter, cut them into crescents with it, if not divide into diamonds or any shape you please; fry these a very pale brown in hot butter; spread on each a little thin mustard, and over that a layer of *rich* cheese; season with a little salt and white pepper; bake in a sharp oven till the cheese is dissolved. Serve hot as possible on a napkin.

CHEESE FRITTERS.

This will do to use up cheese that has become a little dry, although, of course, fresh would be better. Put in a chopping bowl or mortar three ounces of grated cheese, a dessert-spoonful of finely chopped ham (this may be omitted if not liked), three dessert-spoonfuls of finely grated bread-crumbs, a teaspoonful of dry mustard, a piece of butter the size of an egg; a speck of cayenne, and the yolk of an egg beaten. Pound together with a potatoe masher or pestle till smooth and thoroughly mixed; form the balls into paste the size of a walnut; flatten a little, dip them into frying batter (see recipe), and fry a light brown (see Frying). They will take about two minutes to fry.

CHAPTER XXXIII.

SAUCES, SAVORY.

ENGLISH BREAD SAUCE.

The English serve bread sauce with most kinds of game, also with roast chicken and turkey.

Take two ounces of bread-crumbs; be careful there is no crust as the sauce must be very white; put them in half a pint of rich milk, with six peppercorns and a medium-sized onion; let them boil at the back of the stove ten minutes; then take out the onion and pepper corns; stir in a tablespoonful of butter; or two of *thick* cream if you have it; stir till the butter is dissolved; if liked, a suspicion of nutmeg may be added. Serve hot in a sauce tureen. Never prepare this sauce till wanted, as if it stands it will get pappy.

BROWN SAUCE, OR ESPAGNOLE (SPANISH SAUCE) (GOUFFÉ).

This sauce is one of the two sauces called by the French "mother sauces," because these two sauces are the foundation of nearly all others. If you succeed in making them well, you can make the most dainty and most elaborate sounding French sauces which may frighten you to think of, yet which are very easy.

For true Espagnole (I use the French name here, that

when some book orders you to "take half a pint of Espagnole" you may remember the brown sauce you can make so easily is the identical thing) is required good stock or else glaze (see Chapter IV).

Dissolve a piece of glaze the size of a walnut in half a pint of water, or else take a pint of strong soup or stock. Put into it half a carrot, an onion—both cut fine—a bouquet of herbs, and a lump of sugar; boil slowly till reduced to one-half the liquid; then strain, pressing the vegetables to get all the liquid out. Put in another saucepan one ounce of butter, and scant one of flour; let them brown, stirring them to prevent burning; when a light brown, pour the stock to the flour and butter and stir till it is smooth. This is Espagnole. If you have brown flour at hand and use it instead of white, you will not need to wait for the flour and butter to brown.

A SIMPLE AND QUICK BROWN SAUCE.

Cut up an onion, put it in a saucepan with a teaspoonful of butter, fry it brown; put in two cloves, a stick of celery, or six celery seeds, a bouquet of herbs, and a teaspoonful of gelatine; boil all in a pint of water till the gelatine is dissolved; take off the liquid and stir in it a large teaspoonful of Liebig's extract of beef; thicken with brown thickening, and put in half a teaspoonful of salt.

Remember, although good sauces always call for stock, and this may sometimes seem to preclude the possibility of making them, there generally is in most families the means of making stock in the house—the bones from a roast of beef, or of a turkey or chicken, or even a leg of mutton bone, will all, or any, yield half a pint of stock, taking care to break them up as small as possible; add to them a carrot, an onion, and a bouquet of herbs. A little arrangement is to be found at the best hardware stores for cracking up bones, which is a great economy in any family and would soon pay for itself.

The following are a few of the sauces made from brown sauce, and which, solely on account of their name, I think, people living near the great caterers buy by the pint, at a very high price.

BORDELAISE (GOUFFÉ).

Put half a pint of Sauterne wine in a saucepan, boil it down to one gill; put a tablespoonful of chopped shallot blanched (see directions), or onion (a poor substitute), one pinch of pepper, and a pint of brown sauce.

SAUCE PIQUANTE (SIMPLIFIED FROM GOUFFÉ).

Fry or stew half an ounce of shallot or onion chopped, in a dessert-spoonful of vinegar; let it cook until the vinegar is all absorbed—be very careful about this; then put it into three-quarters of a pint of brown sauce (to which you have added a gill of broth or water to allow for the boiling away); add a tablespoonful of chopped cucumber, and one of chopped parsley; cook gently fifteen minutes.

SAUCE POIVRADE.

Dissolve two ounces of butter in a saucepan; a carrot, a turnip, an onion cut in two, also, if to be had, a shallot and two cloves, a sprig of thyme, one of parsley, a bay leaf, a little salt, and two peppercorns; let these all fry until they are a nice brown, stirring them all the time; then add gradually a small cup of claret and half a pint of good brown sauce; simmer gently ten minutes, and remove the scum as it rises; strain and serve very hot.

SAUCE ROBERT.

Fry in a small saucepan three medium-sized onions, chopped *fine*, in a tablespoonful of butter; stir them as they fry, till they are clear and brownish; add to them half a pint of brown sauce and a wineglass of water or broth to allow for the boiling away; boil twenty minutes and strain; then mix one teaspoonful of vinegar in a cup with a teaspoonful of mustard, which stir into the sauce and it is ready to use.

BEURRE NOIR, OR BROWN BUTTER.

Put two ounces of butter in a small saucepan; let it get brown, but not burn; when it is a good color let it cool slightly; then pour in a tablespoonful of vinegar which you have made hot but not boiled; heat both together. If you want it for poached eggs it is ready to use, but for fish it should have a teaspooonful of chopped parsley added.

BROWN THICKENING

Under the name of *Roux* this is given on page 34. White thickening (Blanc) is on the same page.

MINT SAUCE FOR ROAST LAMB.

One tablespoonful of mint leaves, very finely chopped; three tablespoonfuls of vinegar—if very strong, use one-third water, and a dessert-spoonful of sugar; mix two or three hours before using it.

BROWN MUSHROOM SAUCE.

Add to half a pint of brown sauce the liquor from a can of mushrooms and half of the mushrooms; stew five minutes. It is much improved by a glass of sherry, in which case the sauce must be allowed to cook down if it should be too thin. With the mushroom liquor and sherry, stock to make the brown sauce is not indispensable, although a great improvement.

Use with fillet of beef, or roast beef, steak, etc.

TOMATO SAUCE (BLOT).

Put in a stew-pan two ounces of butter, half a bay leaf, two peppercorns, a sprig of thyme, an onion cut up, a sprig of parsley, a dozen medium-sized tomatoes, and two wineglasses of broth or water; stew altogether about an hour; then rub them through a strainer; put a tablespoonful of butter and a *dessert*-spoonful of flour in a small saucepan; stir together till they bubble, then pour on the tomato juice and stir till smooth.

WHITE SAUCES.

When sauces are thickened with eggs, it is safer after they are added to stand the saucepan in another containing boiling water, and stir it in that, until it reaches the boiling point; remember it must not boil or it will break; yet if it does not reach the boiling point, the eggs will not thicken.

BUTTER SAUCE

Is the foundation for several well-known white French sauces. It will be observed that the first step is always the same—equal proportions of butter and flour stirred together over the fire until the flour is cooked; then milk is added for white sauce, veal or chicken stock for béchamel, water for butter sauce. On these foundations are several variations: eggs and oil make butter sauce into Hollandaise; mushrooms and eggs make it into velouté or allemande; a glass of white wine makes it poulette.

When butter sauce, or white sauce is to be served simply, more butter may be added in proportion to the quantity of flour; the butter will only make the sauce more rich, not thicker or thinner; the flour should be one tablespoonful, or ounce, to half a pint of liquid. A recipe for very rich white sauce is given in the first part of this book. That sauce cannot be improved upon for instant use, but butter or white sauce made very rich, will break if left standing many minutes. The best proportions for a sauce that is to be kept hot, is one ounce of butter, one ounce of flour to half a pint of liquid. If wanted richer than this, stir in one or two ounces of butter at the *last moment*.

BUTTER SAUCE, SIMPLE.

One ounce of butter, one ounce of flour; put the butter in a small, thick saucepan, marbleized, or iron (never use tin for sauce); when melted put in the flour, stirring it, let it bubble, stirring all the time till it is a fine yellow, it takes one minute usually; then pour in half a pint of hot water and a saltspoonful of salt. Using milk instead of water makes it a simple white sauce.

ALLEMANDE SAUCE.

One ounce of butter put in a thick saucepan; when melted add one ounce of flour, stir them, let them bubble one minute; then pour in—stirring all the while—half a pint of hot broth or white stock, or if you have not it, hot water and the liquid from a can of mushooms. Let it boil, take from the fire, wait a minute and stir in gradually the yolks of three eggs, a saltspoon of salt, a quarter one of pepper; return it to the fire, stirring carefully; it must get to the boiling point, or the eggs will not be cooked, yet on no account boil, or it will curdle; when it is off the fire, stir in a tablespoonful more butter. If it should be too thick, add a *very little broth* or hot water.

SAUCE SUPREME.

Make an *Allemande* as above; add to it two tablespoonfuls of butter and three of stock; stir, and bring it to the boiling point at once; squeeze in a few drops of lemon juice; use at once.

POULETTE.

Make *Allemande* sauce and add to it a glass of white wine. If anything is to be cooked in it, as sweetbreads or chicken, leave out the eggs till last: they are sometimes omitted altogether.

CAPER SAUCE.

To half a pint of butter sauce put a dessert-spoonful of capers—not chopped, it spoils the appearance—and a teaspoonful of the vinegar, a saltspoonful of salt, and a quarter one of pepper (white).

BÉCHAMEL NO. 1.

One ounce of butter put in a thick saucepan to melt; add one ounce of flour, let them bubble a minute, stirring all the time; pour to it half a pint of hot strained white stock which has been well flavored with vegetables; stir it and let it boil till quite thick—five minutes perhaps—then add a gill of very thick cream. If the stock was seasoned add very little salt, or the butter may have been salt enough. The stock used must be quite free from color or sediment.

This sauce, so simply made, makes many delicious dishes ; any white meat can be warmed over in it, or it can be used to mask boiled chickens or turkey. Pour it over them while hot ; and when cold it will lay over them like a white jelly, making a very elegant dish if properly and carefuly put on. The bird should be as completely and smoothly covered as a cake is with icing.

BECHAMEL NO. 2, FOR FISH.

Boil the bones and trimmings of fish (or else use a flounder for the purpose) in a quart of water in which you have a bouquet of sweet herbs, a bay leaf, a piece of carrot, half a dozen peppercorns, and a small teaspoonful of salt ; boil till there is only half a pint of stock ; strain through a cloth, and pour it on to a tablespoonful of butter and flour that have been cooked together, as for white sauce, stirring carefully ; when thick and smooth stir in a gill of cream ; use as a sauce for fish where directed.

OYSTER SAUCE, WHITE.

Open two dozen oysters, carefully preserve the liquor; stir one ounce of butter and one ounce of flour together over the fire until they bubble; pour the strained oyster liquor into a half-pint measure and as much cream or milk as will fill it; make this hot and put it to the butter and flour, stirring all the while; when it boils put in the oysters, leave them only till they are firm and plump; when the edges begin to curl they are done; add half the juice of a small lemon, a quarter of a saltspoonful of pepper, and salt as may be required.

This sauce is excellent with turkey.

OYSTER SAUCE, BROWN.

Make half a pint of brown sauce; add the liquor strained from two dozen oysters; boil together till of the right thickness (the oyster liquor will have thinned it), then drop in the oysters, let them simmer till the edges curl; take the sauce from the fire instantly.

It is English fashion to send this sauce to table with beefsteak.

SOUBISE OR ONION SAUCE.

Boil medium sized onions tender, chop them up quickly, put them into cold water while you make half a pint of white sauce, then put a half saltspoonful of white pepper in it; *drain* the onions, add them to the sauce, and if you have it, a little cream; let them cook together ten minutes and serve.

If you have the white sauce ready when the onions are chopped, you need not throw them into cold water; it is only to prevent them getting dark in color.

HOLLANDAISE SAUCE, (GOUFFÉ).

Put in a saucepan two tablespoonfuls of vinegar, with a saltspoonful of salt, and half one of pepper (white), let it boil down to one dessert-spoonful. Take it from the fire, add two tablespoonfuls of cold water, and yolks of two eggs beaten; put on the fire again, stirring till it begins to thicken (take care it does not boil); take it off the fire again, add a piece of butter the size of a walnut, stir till melted; replace on the fire one minute, take off again; put another piece of butter the same size, stirring until the butter melts and becomes incorporated with the eggs; replace again on the fire, do this until four ounces of butter have been used and the sauce looks like a thick yellow mayonnaise. Never add more butter until the last is thoroughly blended; and when you put in the third piece, put in a tablespoonful of cold water, to prevent it turning.

You will observe that the whole process is very much like making a hot mayonnaise, using butter instead of oil; the reason for the frequent taking off and putting on the fire, is because the eggs must be at *boiling point*, yet not boil; after each fresh piece of butter, they are cooled; they must then be brought back to the same degree, if they were left on the stove the butter would oil.

It sounds much more complicated than it is, and *this* Hollandaise is the one found in all fine French cooking; but it is not the one commonly used in this country and in England, which is as follows:

DUTCH OR HOLLANDAISE SAUCE (SIMPLE).

Make half a pint of *butter sauce* as directed, then stir in *gradually* the beaten yolks of three eggs and two tablespoonfuls of oil, putting it in drop by drop just as you would for mayonnaise; when thick and smooth, put in a dessert-spoonful of lemon juice, a saltspoonful of salt, and half one of white pepper. Some mix with the lemon juice before adding it a teaspoonful of dry mustard.

You will observe this recipe is simply a combination

of mayonnaise and butter sauce, and when cold can be used as a salad dressing by those who do not care for so rich a sauce as mayonnaise.

GREEN DUTCH SAUCE,

Is simply Hollandaise sauce with sufficient parsley juice to color it green. Pound the leaves of fresh parsley and squeeze the juice through muslin. Stir it into the sauce the last thing.

MAYONNAISE.

Stir the yolk of one egg in a bowl for one minute, then add oil drop by drop, stirring all the time; when once the oil and egg have thickened, and taken an opaque creamy consistency, the oil may be put in more freely. Yet always be careful to see it well blended before adding more.

When it gets very thick, add a few drops of vinegar, then more oil, till you have as much as you require; the vinegar must depend on individual taste; half a gill of vinegar is usually enough for half a pint of oil. Add salt and pepper last; many mix a teaspoonful of dry mustard with the egg at starting, but although a pleasant addition, it does not belong to mayonnaise proper, but to tartar sauce.

N. B.—This sauce can be made more surely when bowl, egg and oil are ice cold; in warm weather make it in a cool room.

TARTAR SAUCE, NO. 1.

Make some mayonnaise, put into a bowl a teaspoonful of dry mustard, mix with a tablespoonful of the mayonnaise till smooth. Add a tablespoonful of finely chopped shallots, a teaspoonful each of tarragon and chervil; mix all together, and add to the mayonnaise.

TARTAR SAUCE, NO. 2.

It is often difficult to obtain the herbs used in French tartar sauce—therefore this substitute is commonly used; a tablespoonful of finely chopped parsley, one dessert-spoonful of capers, one of finely chopped pickled cucumbers, and half a one of onion or shallot. Add these to half a pint of mayonnaise, or half to half the quantity. Mustard as in last recipe.

SWEET SAUCES.

ALMOND SAUCE.

Take two ounces of almond paste, boil half a pint of rich milk, pour a little on the almond paste at first, to soften and moisten it. When it is well mixed with the back of a fork, pour on the rest of the boiling milk; mix a teaspoonful of flour with a little cold milk; pour this to the almonds and milk. Let it boil two minutes, remove from the fire, wait one minute, then stir in the yolk of an egg; stir altogether over the fire till it comes to boiling point. Add sugar to taste, and serve for any sweet pudding.

HARD SAUCE.

Wash half a cup of butter till the salt is nearly all out of it; then beat it, gradually adding a cup of powdered sugar; and the beaten white of one egg; when it is all very light and white, flavor either with a teaspoonful of vanilla powder or extract, or with a tablespoonful of wine.

LEMON SAUCE, (NEW YORK COOKING SCHOOL).

One cup of sugar, half a cup of water, the rind (pared off very thinly) of two lemons, with the strained juice; boil all together ten minutes; beat the yolk of three eggs. Strain the syrup, stir the the eggs into it, set the saucepan in another of boiling water, and beat rapidly till thick and smooth; remove from the water, and beat five minutes.

CHANDÔT. CARÊME'S CELEBRATED PUDDING SAUCE.

Mix half a pint of sherry, with four ounces of sugar and two eggs well beaten in a bowl, which set in a saucepan of boiling water; beat rapidly with an egg-beater till thick and smooth.

ENGLISH BRANDY SAUCE FOR PLUM PUDDINGS.

A tablespoonful of butter stirred in a saucepan over the fire, with two teaspoonfuls of flour, till they bubble. Stir into them a gill of water and half a gill of brandy.

POLKA SAUCE.

Beat three ounces of butter, with a cup of powdered sugar, till they are very light and foamy; set the bowl in boiling water, make three glasses of sherry hot, add it gradually to the butter and sugar, beating all the time; do not cease beating till all are at the boiling point. Then serve with ice-cold polka pudding.

VANILLA SAUCE.

Quarter of a cup of butter, a cup of water, and one of sugar, boil together; remove from the fire, have two eggs well beaten, pour the hot mixture to them and then stir together over the fire till thick; if you do this in a bowl set in boiling water, there is less danger of curdling the eggs. Add one teaspoonful of vanilla powder or extract and serve.

FRUIT SAUCE.

Sauce from fresh fruit is made by stewing the fruit, cherries, raspberries, etc., in an equal quantity of water and half a pint of sugar to each pint of water; when very tender, pulp through a strainer. It may be thickened with a little cornstarch if desired.

CHAPTER XXXIV.

CAKES.

SPONGE JELLY CAKE.

Beat three whole eggs ten minutes by the clock, with a cup of sugar; they should then look like thick cream beaten, a full cup of flour, and a teaspoonful of baking powder; spread on tins, and bake five minutes in a *very hot* oven; the whole success of the cake depends on the oven. It is very like real sponge if right.

Spread with jelly, or cream, whipped and flavored; put one layer on the other, and sift powdered sugar over.

CUP CAKE.

Beat a cup of butter, or one-half lard, to a cream, with two cups of sugar. Grate in the peel of a lemon, beat the yolks of three eggs, stir them in, then sift in three cups of flour, using just milk enough to make it a very thick batter; when the flour is in, whip the whites firm and add them, put in a pinch of salt, and two teaspoonfuls of baking powder; bake in a buttered tin in a quick oven. I always keep a piece of cardboard (part of an old paper box will do) to cover over cakes the first part of the time they are in the oven; this prevents the heavy streak, that is sometimes caused by the crust forming before the cake has well risen.

FRUIT CUP CAKE.

Make by above recipe, only have ready a cup of fruit, currants and citron or anything you like, well floured and made quite warm. Add them last, just stirring them in, and get the cake into the oven quickly.

N. B.—Fruit put in without flouring it will sink to the bottom, so it will if put in cold, or if the cake is stirred much after it is added. A glass of wine is a great addition to either of these cakes.

SPONGE CAKE.

Beat the whites of five eggs till they are solid, add the yolks to them, stirring very gently; grate the rind of a small lemon and squeeze in the juice of half. Sift in eight ounces of powdered sugar, and four of sifted flour, add a pinch of salt. Stir very gently after the flour is added, and only enough to mix it. Line a tin with buttered paper, and pour the cake into it; bake forty-five minutes in a brisk oven. Cover the cake the first half hour. When you take it out keep it from all drafts, or it will fall.

POUND CAKE, (VERY RICH).

One pound of butter washed in rose-water if you want it very nice; beat it to a cream with the yolks of eight eggs and a pound of sugar, add a glass of wine and one of brandy, with a tablespoonful of rose-water unless the butter was washed in it. When very creamy, stir in a pound of sifted flour, and the whites of eight eggs, beaten to a firm froth.

Bake in a tin lined with buttered paper; it requires a steady slow oven and will take an hour and a half; cover for the first hour.

FRUIT POUND CAKE.

Make by foregoing recipe; but prepare a pound of very well cleaned and dried fruit, shake two tablespoonfuls of flour through it, then sift out all that does not adhere.

Make the fruit very warm and add the last thing.

PLAIN ICING.

Mix a pound of powdered sugar with the whites of two eggs, the juice of half a lemon, a dessert-spoonful of rose-water. Simply stir till smooth, and spread over the cake with a knife dipped in cold water.

FONDANT ICING.

This has taken the place of the old-fashioned frosting except for plum or pound cake. To make it, see "Fondant," in the first part of this book, page 92. Melt the fondant by standing the bowl containing it, in a saucepan of boiling water and stirring it till it is like cream, taking care none of the water boils into it; flavor and color as you please; spread it on the warm cake like other icing.

INDEX.

	PAGE
Albert pudding	203
Allemande sauce	224
Almond creams	93
Almond sauce	230
Altering recipes	111, 112
Apple pie, No. 1	210
" " No. 2	210
Apple pudding, English	136, 201
Asparagus, to boil	66
Salad	197
Soups	142, 148
Baba cake	86
Small	87
Syrup for	87
Balls, egg	144
Forcemeat	131
Baked, black fish	155
Blue fish	152
Tomatoes	138
Batter bread	121
Batter for frying, à la Carême	59
" " " Provençale	60
Batter fruit puddings	202
Béchamel, No. 1	225
" No. 2	226
Filet de sole en	151
BEEF	
Au gratin	75
Beefsteak, to broil	60
Stewed	175
Bœuf à la jardiniere	74
Breakfast dish of	78
Filet, au Chateaubriand	49
Filet roast	179
Fritadella	81
Miroton of	76
Olives of	79
Pseudo beefsteak	75
Ragout of cold	78
Salmi of cold	73
Roast of	178
Simplest way to warm	77
Stock	68
Sirloin to make two dishes	49
To warm a large piece	78
To garnish	179
Beets, cream of	148
Beurre noir	222
Birds, small on toast	193

	PAGE
Biscuit, egg	121
Quick	122
Biscuit, glacé à la Charles Dickens	85
Biscuit, glacé à la Thackeray	85
Blackberry tart	209
Blackfish, baked	155
Blanc, or white thickening	34
Blanch, to	133
Bluefish, baked	152
BOILING, Chapter on	65
Boil to	
Asparagus	66, 136
Cabbage	65, 136
Carrots	137
Cauliflower	135
Codfish	150
Filet de sole	151
Fowl	189
Ham	65
Lobster	198
Meats	65
Onions	139
Peas	136
Puddings	201
Salmon	150
String beans	136
Sweet corn	138
Turkey	188
Bordelaise sauce, Gouffé's	221
Bouchées de dames	88
Brains, au beurre noir	159
Braised, fowl	186
Turkey	187
Brandy sauce, English	231
BREAD, Chapter on	12
Batter bread	121
Baking	14
Breakfast breads	119
Cause of failure	14
" of thick crust	15
Compressed yeast	15
Corn bread	120
Crumbs for frying	56
Dough to keep	106
Pie, crust of	97
Kneading of	14
Oven, heating of	14
Rules for rising of	14

	PAGE
Sauce	219
Soufflée	20
To set sponge for	13
Breakfast dish	78
Salad	200
Brioche	18
Jockey Club recipe for	19
For summer pastry	19, 20
Broiling, General rules for meats	60
Chicken	61
Broiled prairie hen	192
Partridge	192
Quail	193
Salmon	150
Brown butter	222
Flour	34
Mushroom sauce	223
Oyster sauce	227
Sauce, or Espagnole	71, 219, 220
Roux, or thickening	34
Butter, brown	222
Maître d'hôtel	32
Montpellier	33
Ravigotte	33
Sauce	136, 223
Cabbage, to boil	65
CAKES	
Baba	86
Bouchées de dames	88
Cup	233
Fruit cup	234
Jelly	233
Fruit pound	234
Pound	234
Savarin	88
Icing for	92, 235
Calf's brains, au beurre noir	159
Head, à la tortue	157
with Hollandaise sauce	157
Tongue stewed	158
Canopées of cheese	218
CANDIES	
Chocolate creams	94
Cream almonds	93
Cream walnuts	93
Fondant	92
Panaché	93
Punch drops	94
Simple French	92
Vanilla almond cream	92
Walnut cream	92
Caper sauce	225
Capon, to roast	190
Cardinal salad	197
Carp, stewed	153
French mode	154
Carrots, to boil	137
Cones of	137
Cases, for patties	170
Cauliflower, to boil	135
Soup	148
Caramel for coloring	126
Celeraic	54

	PAGE
Celery seed for soup	106
Celery cream soup	68
Cheese canopées	218
Fondu	216
Fritters	218
Straws	217
Cherry pudding	202
CHICKEN	
Boiled	189
Broiled	60
Cold	49
Croquettes	162
Fricassee	165, 166
Fritters	164
Kromesquis	164
Patties	173
Pie	38
Rissoles	163
Roast	48, 186
Use of feet	48
Preparation of	184
Chops, breaded	161
Christmas puddings	205
Clinkers, to remove	107
Cod	150
Cocoanut pies	212
Coloring	126, 95
Company to lunch	44
Cream patties	212
Cream soups	148
Croquettes of chicken	162
Lobster	168
Salmon	168
Cromesquies or kromeskies of chicken	164
Of cold lamb	75
Croutons for garnishing	129
Crumbs for frying	56
Cup cakes	233
Cutlets, veal	160
Lobster	168
Venison	195
Cucumber and onion ragout	102
Curaçoa, to make	89
Curry	108
Daube, to prepare meat à la	129
Devilled meat	80
Dishes without meat	102
Dresden patties	173
Dripping, to clarify	59
Duck, salmi of	166
Roast	189
Dutch sauce, green	229
Egg biscuit	121
Egg balls for soup	144
Eggs fried in balls	129
English apple pudding	201
Brandy sauce	231
Christmas pudding	205
Fruit tarts	209
Mock turtle soups	142
Muffins	122
Raised pies	38

	PAGE		PAGE
Veal and ham pies	38	Sage and onion, for goose, pork and ducks	132
Windsor pie	36	Veal	132
ENTRÉES		Fowl, boiled	189
Calf's brains au beurre noir	159	Braised	186
Calf's head, Hollandaise sauce	157	Roast	186
Calf's head, à la tortue	157	Frangipani cream	213
Calf's tongue, stewed	158	Tartlets	26
Chicken croquettes	162	French herbs	113
Fricassee, No. 1	165	Friandises	84
" No. 2	166	Fricassee chicken, No. 1	165
Rissoles	163	" " No. 2	166
Fritters	164	Veal	166
Patties	173	Fritadella of cold meat	81
Kromeskies	164	Fritters, cheese	218
Dresden patties	173	Chicken	164
Lamb chops breaded	161	Fruit, batter pudding	202
Lobster croquettes	168	Cup cake	234
Cutlets	168	Pound cake	235
Patties	171	Sauces	232
Mutton chops breaded	161	FRYING	
Oyster patties	172	Batter for	59
Salmi of duck	166	Provençale	60
Of cold meat	73	Crumbing for	56
Of game	166	Oil for	58
Salmon croquettes	168	To clarify fat for	59
Patties	173	To test heat of fat	57
Sweetbreads fried	159	Croquettes	163
With mushrooms	159	Filet de sole	56
Simple dish of	160	Fritters	164
Veal fricassee	166	Oysters	57
Cutlets	160	Parsley	128
Variations	164	Smelts	154
Fire-bricks, to remove clinkers	107	Sweetbreads	159
Family soups	141	Galantine	39
Feuilletonage	23	GAME	
Filet of beef	179	Epicure's way of preparing	194
Filet of veal stuffed	180	Grouse	191
With mushrooms or oysters	181	Partridge	191
FISH		Prairie Hen	191
Black fish, baked	155	Quick way to cook small birds	194
Blue fish, baked	152	Salmi of	166
Broiled salmon, caper sauce	150	Small birds on toast	193
Carp, stewed, No. 1	153	Snipe	193
" " No. 2	154	Woodcock	193
Cod, oyster sauce	150	Venison	194, 195
Halibut, caper sauce	151	Garnishing	127
Filet de sole in béchamel	151	Garlic	108
Same fried	56	Glaze	30
Au gratin	154	To glaze ham, tongue, etc	32
Salmon, boiled, green Dutch sauce	150	Gouffé's pot-au-feu	68
Smelts	154	Bordelaise sauce	221
Fisherman's soup	145	Hollandaise sauce	227
Flavoring	70	Omelet soufflée	214
Flaming omelet	214	Soufflée à la Vanille	214
Flounders, to bone	56	Rules for ovens	27
" as filet de sole	56	Grating nutmegs	105
Fondant	92	Gravy	29, 63
For icing	235	Grease, to clear soup of	142
Fondu	216	Green Dutch sauce	229
Forequarter of mutton	101	Green pea soups	149
Forcemeat, chestnut	131	Hard sauce	230
Oyster	132	Haricot of mutton	175

	PAGE		PAGE
Hash	97	Meat, to keep	106
Head, calves, Hollandaise sauce	157	Salad	52
" à la tortue	157	Mephistophelian sauce, Soyer's	81
Heart, beef	100	Miroton of beef	76
Sheep's	99	Montpellier butter	33
Hollandaise sauce, No. 1	227	Mock turtle soup	142
" " No. 2	228	Clear	143
Iced claret soup	149	Thick	143
Icing plain	235	Muffins, English	122
Fondant	235	Corn	121
Iced pudding, polka	203	Mulligatawny soup	144
Queen Mab	204	**MUTTON**	
Iced soufflée	85	Chops breaded	161
" à la Byron	84	Forequarter of	101
Jelly cake	233	Haricot of	175
Jellied fish or oysters	41	Neck of	101
Jelly for cold chickens	47	Leg of	52
Jelly from pork	31	Roast	179
Kerosene lamps	107	Saddle of	180
Keeping meat	105	Mushroom soup, white	147
Poultry	107	Fillet of veal with	181
Dough	106	Omelet	125
Kensington, South, rough puff paste	169	Sauce	223
		Powder	29
Kitchen conveniences	114	Nutmegs, best way to grate	105
Kreuznach horns	16	Noyeau	90
Kringles	17	Omelet, easy	45
Kromesquies (or Cromesquies)	164	French	124
Of chicken	164	Flaming	214
Of lamb	75	Ham	125
Lamb, cromesquies of	75	Mushroom	125
Roast	180	Oyster	125
Lamps	107	Soufflée	214
Larding needle	112	Tomato	124
Larding	129	Onion soup, maigre	103
Leg of mutton à la soubise	52	Onions stewed	139
Boiled	52	Spring stewed	139
Roast	179	Sauce or soubise	227
Lemon pie, No. 1	210	Ornamenting meat pies	37
" No. 2	211	Ovens, Gouffé's, rules for heating	14
" rich, No. 3	211	Oysters	27
Pudding	203	Bisque of	146
Peels	106	Forcemeat of	132
Sauce	231	In Jelly	41
To keep	105	Omelet	125
Lettuce salad	196	Patties	172
Little dinners	50	Sauce, brown	227
Liver, sheep's	98	White	226
Lobster, to boil	198	To fry	57
Bisque of	146	Ox cheek	100
Croquettes of	168	Partridge, to broil	192
Cutlets	168	Roast	191
Patties	171	Parsley, in winter	113
Salads	196	Seed for soup	106
Luncheons, Chapter on	35	To fry	128
Macaroni with veal	182	Pastry, Chapter on	22
Maitre d'Hotel butter	32	To handle	24
Management in small families	47	Tablets	26
Maraschino, to make	90	Flaky family paste	208
Marrow, from soup bone	98	Rough puff paste	169
Mayonnaise sauce	229	*Pate royale* for soups	141
With jelly	42	Patty cases	170
Of potatoes	199		

Index.

	PAGE
PATTIES	
Cream	212
Chicken	173
Dresden	173
Frangipani	213
Lobster	171
Oyster	172
Salmon	173
To fill	172
Peas, to boil	136
Soup, green	149
Maigre	103
PIES	
Apple pie, No. 1	210
" " No. 2	210
Chicken, to eat cold	33
Cocoanut, No. 1	211
" No. 2	212
English raised	38
Lemon, No. 1	210
" No. 2	211
" No. 3 (rich)	211
Sea	176
Veal and ham	38
Windsor	36
Piquante sauce	221
Plain dishes	174
Poivrade sauce	221
Potatoes, boiled	66
Mayonnaise of	199
Salads	54, 199
Snow	45
Soup, maigre	103
To warm over	46
Pot-au-feu	68
Pot-roasts	99
Potted meats	43
Polka pudding	203
Pork, for jelly	31
Roast loin of	183
Forcemeat for	132
Poulette sauce	225
Pound cake	234
Fruit	235
Poultry, to prepare	184
To stuff	185
Preparation of game	191
Poultry	184
Vegetables	135
Prairie hen, roast	191
Broiled	192
PUDDINGS	
Albert	203
Apple, English	201
Batter, with fruit	202
Cherry	202
Christmas, No. 1	205
" No. 2	206
To mix	206
General directions for boiled	201
Lemon	203
Polka	203
Queen Mab	204

	PAGE
Troy	204
Puffs, buttermilk	123
Puff paste	22
Puff paste, rough	169
Punch drops	78
QUAILS	
Broiled	193
Roasted	193
Queen Mab pudding	204
Quick biscuit	122
Ragout, of cold meat	78
Of cucumber and onion	102
Ramaquins	217
Raminoles, Soyer's	216
Raspberry tart	209
Ravigotte	33
Recipes, to alter	111, 112
Remarks, preliminary	1–12
On altering recipes	111, 112
On boiling	65
On bread making	12
On frying	54
On garnishing	127
On kitchen and servants	114
On little dinners	50
On luncheons	35
On maigre dishes	104
On management in small families	47
On sauces and flavoring	70
On soups	67, 140
On table prejudices	108
On true economy in buying meat	99
On roasting	62
Rissoles, chicken, etc	163
Rissolettes	25
ROAST	
Beef	178
Capon	190
Chicken	186
Duck	189
Fillet of beef	179
Fillet of veal, stuffed	180
with mushrooms or oysters	181
Fowl	186
Goose	189
Lamb	180
Leg of mutton	179
Loin of pork	183
Loin of veal	183
Partridge	191
Prairie hen	191
Quail	193
Saddle of mutton	180
Shoulder of veal, stuffed	182
Turkey	187
Veal with macaroni	182
Venison	194
Robert sauce	222
Rolls, soufflée breakfast	120
Fine	15
Rough puff paste	169

Index.

	PAGE
Roux	34
Royal paste for soup	141
Rusks	16
Sage and onion forcemeat	132
SALADS	
Anchovy	197
Asparagus	197
Breakfast, Murreys	200
Cardinal	197
Celeraic	54
Chicken	198
Cold meat	52
Lettuce	196
Lobster	198
Mayonnaise of potato	199
Potato	19, 199
Pork in	199
Tomato, No. 1	200
" No. 2	200
Veal in	199
Salamander, substitute for	112
Salmi	
Of duck	166
Of cold meat	73
Of game	166
Sauce	167
Salmon, boiled	150
Croquettes	168
Patties	173
Steaks broiled	150
Savarin cake	88
SAUCES	
Almond	230
Allemande	224
Béchamel, No. 1	225
" No. 2	226
Beurre noir	222
Bordelaise (Gouffé)	221
Bread	219
Brown, or espagnole	71, 219
No. 2, simple and quick	220
Brown thickening for	34
Brown mushroom	223
Brown oyster	227
Butter, brown	222
" White	224
Caper	225
Chandôt (Carême's)	231
English brandy	231
Flavoring for	70
Fruit	231
Green Dutch	229
Hard	230
Hollandaise (Gouffé's)	227
" No. 2	228
Mayonnaise, No. 1	229
" No. 2	42
Mephistophelian	81
Oyster brown	227
" White	226
Polka	231
Soubise or onion	227
Supreme	225

	PAGE
Salmi	167
Tartar, No. 1	229
" No. 2	230
Tomato	223
Vanilla	231
White thickening for	34
Scotch scones	120
Scones	120
Sea pie	176
Smelts, to fry	154
Small birds, quick way to cook	193, 194
Snipe on toast	193
Sole, filet de	56, 151
SOUFFLEE	
à la vanilla	214
Bread	20
Iced	84
à la Byron	85
Omelette	214
Rolls	119
Soup bone	96
SOUPS.	
Asparagus	148
Gouffé's pot-an-feu, or beef stock for	68
Bisque of lobster	146
" of clams	146
" of oysters	146
Claret soup, iced	149
Clear soup	140
How to clear	140
Clear vegetable	141
Coloring for	126, 67
Consommée à la royale	141
Cream of beets	148
" of cauliflower	148
" of celery	68
" of spinach	148
Egg balls for	144
Family soup	141
French fisherman's	145
Mock-Turtle, English, clear	142
" Thick	144
Mock-Turtle, No. 2	144
Mulligatawny	144
Mushroom white	147
Onion	103
Pease, green	149
" dried	103
Potato	103
To remove grease from	142
Vermicelli	140
Spinach, to boil	138
Sponge cake	234
Sponge jelly cake	233
Stewed tomatoes	138
Carp, No. 1	153
" No. 2	154
Beefsteak	175
Onions	139
Spring onions	139
Stew, Irish	174

Index.

	PAGE
Stock, beef	68
Veal	147
Straws, cheese	217
String beans, to boil	136
To cut	136
Stuffing for veal or fish	132
How to stuff	133
Sweet breads, to fry	159
Stewed with mushrooms	159
Simple dish of	160
Sugar, to boil	91
Tainted meat, to restore	107
Tartar sauce, No. 1	229
" " No. 2	230
Tarts, English fruit	209
Blackberry	209
Raspberry and currant	209
Cherry and currant	209
Thickening, brown or roux	34
White or blanc	34
Tomato, baked	138
Omelet of	124
Salad	200
Stewed	28
Sauce	223
Tongue, calf's stewed	158
Trussing, poultry and game	185, 191
Turkey, boiled	188
Braised	187
Roast	187
Turnips, to boil	137
Cones of	137
Tutti frutti candy	92
Vanilla almond cream	92
Sauce	231
Soufflée	214
Variations on dishes	164
VEAL	
Cutlets	160
Fricassee	166
Loin roasted	183
Roast fillet	180

	PAGE
Same with mushrooms or oysters	181
With macaroni	182
Stuffing for	132
VEGETABLES	
Asparagus	66, 136
Cabbage	65, 136
Cauliflower	135
Carrots	137
Onions	139
Peas	136
Potatoes	66
Spinach	138
Spring onions	139
String beans	136
Sweet corn	138
To cut vegetables	135
To make strong vegetables milder	106
To prepare	135
VENISON	
Cutlets	195
Roast haunch of	194
Steaks	195
Sauce for	195
Vermicelli soup	140
Warming over. Chapter on	72
What to do with the scraps	45
Where to buy articles not in general use	112
Why meat does not brown in cooking	62
Why you fail with bread	15
Why it has a thick crust	14
Why you fail in puff paste	22
Windsor pie	36
White asparagus soup	148
Oyster sauce	226
Mushroom soup	147
Sauce, No. 1	71
" No. 2	223
Thickening	34

www.ingramcontent.com/pod-product-compliance
Lightning Source LLC
Chambersburg PA
CBHW021404230426
43666CB00006B/633